Target Writing & Grammar Skills

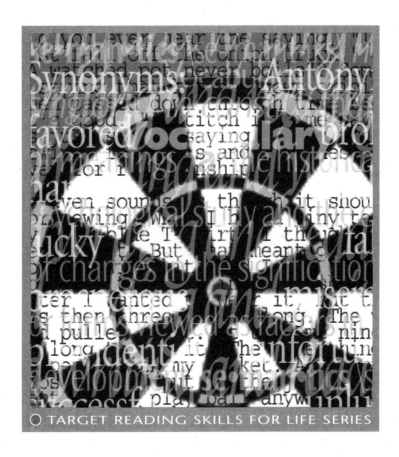

O TARGET READING SKILLS FOR LIFE SERIES

AGS
PUBLISHING

Circle Pines, Minnesota 55014-1796
800-328-2560
www.agsnet.com

Acknowledgements

"The Heroine of Kapiti" as retold by Shirley Climo. First published in *Cricket Magazine,*
July 1983. Reprinted by permission of Shirley Climo.

Cover Design

Sarah Bennett

Photo and Illustration Credits

Page 6, © George Lee White/CORBIS; p. 10, © Michael Keller/CORBIS; p. 14 (all), Roberta Collier-Morales/Portfolio Solutions; p. 18, © Bill Broadhurst/Frank Lane Picture Agency/CORBIS; p. 28, © Kevin Shafer/CORBIS; p. 29, Joel Snyder/Portfolio Solutions; p. 34, © Anthony Bannister/Gallo Images/CORBIS; p. 37, Judy King Rieniets; p. 48, © Photodisc; p. 68, © Meehan Military Posters; p. 74, © Bettmann/CORBIS; p. 80, © CORBIS; p. 88, Judy King Rieniets; p. 92, Joel Snyder/Portfolio Solutions; p. 93 (all), Joel Snyder/Portfolio Solutions; p. 108, Joel Snyder/Portfolio Solutions

Publisher's Project Staff

Associate Director, Product Development: Teri Mathews; Senior Editor: Julie Maas; Development Assistant: Bev Johnson; Design Manager: Nancy Condon; Senior Designer: Daren Hastings; Technical Specialist: Laura Henrichsen; Designer/Project Coordinator: Katie Sonmor; Purchasing Agent: Mary Kaye Kuzma; Senior Marketing Manager/Curriculum: Brian Holl

Development and editorial services by Straight Line Editorial Development, Inc.
Art direction by Sally Brewer Lawrence

© 2003 AGS Publishing
4201 Woodland Road, Circle Pines, MN 55014-1796
800-328-2560
www.agsnet.com

AGS Publishing is a trademark of American Guidance Service, Inc.

Printed in the United States of America

Product Number 93724
ISBN 0-7854-3374-0

A 0 9 8 7 6 5 4 3 2

CONTENTS

CONTENTS

Welcome!

Writing is like anything else that matters. In order to be good at it, you have to practice. *Target Writing & Grammar* will help you become a better writer.

Here are some of the things this book will teach you how to do:

- **Write better sentences.** Even the longest piece of writing is made up of sentences. Knowing how to write good sentences is the first step to becoming a better writer.

- **Write solid paragraphs.** Putting sentences together into a paragraph is an important writing skill. This book will show you how to write paragraphs that are clear and powerful. It's easier than you think!

- **Write longer pieces.** Stories, research papers, letters, and directions—each kind of writing is different. This book will show you how to plan, organize, and polish many different kinds of writing.

- **Choose and use strategies for writing.** This book will teach you some strategies that can help you tackle any writing task, big or small.

- **Use words correctly when writing.** No one likes feeling confused! Help your readers understand what you're saying by using nouns, verbs, pronouns, and other kinds of words correctly.

- **Learn the mechanics of writing.** It's important to use commas, periods, and other kinds of punctuation correctly. This book will show you how.

With practice and a little help from the lessons in this book, you'll be writing like a pro in no time!

WRITING STRATEGY TIPS

Likc any task, writing is best approached with a good plan. Here are some tips:

BEFORE YOU WRITE...

- **Consider your audience and purpose.** Think about why you are writing and who you are writing for.

- **Brainstorm.** When you write, you have a world of ideas to choose from! Think about (and list) some different possibilities for topics. Then pick the idea you like best.

- **Organize your ideas.** Make a visual plan for what you want to say. Put your ideas in an idea web, an outline, a time line, or a story map.

AS YOU WRITE...

- **Don't stress about little things!** In your first draft, just try to get your ideas down on paper. You will have a chance to go back and fix any mistakes later.

- **Stay focused.** Remember what your purpose for writing is. Look back at your visual organizer to help you stay on track.

AFTER YOU WRITE...

- **Reread and improve.** Make sure your sentences are correctly written. Make sure your ideas are in an order that makes sense. If not, change things around. (Sometimes a partner can help you revise.)

- **Check grammar, spelling, and punctuation.** If you're not sure of a word's spelling, look it up in a dictionary. When you use a computer to write, spell check your paper before printing it out.

PROOFREADING TIPS

Proofreading is the final step in writing a paper. To proofread is to read carefully to find mistakes and fix them. Here are some tips:

- **Go slowly.** It's impossible to check your writing for every kind of mistake in one reading. Read once for grammar and spelling. Read a second time for punctuation.

- **Circle and check.** On your first reading, circle every word you think you misspelled. Then go back and check these words in a dictionary. (If you're writing with a computer, be sure to use the spell checker.)

- **Mark clearly.** Mark every mistake clearly so you know what to fix and how to fix it. The proofreader's marks below will help.

Proofreader's Marks

MARK		EXAMPLE	
check spelling	(sp)	I (herd) a loud noise.	(sp)
add something	∧	I heard ∧ loud noise.	a ∧
take something out	⌐	I heard a nasty loud noise.	⌐
make a capital	≡	i heard a loud noise.	
make lowercase	/	I heard a Ḽoud noise.	
switch the order	(tr)	I heard (loud/a) noise.	(tr)

Introduction

Who Needs Sentences?

You do! Here's why. Say you write these words in a list to yourself.

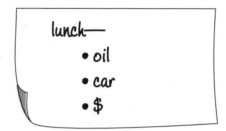

You know just what these words mean: "When I go to lunch, I need to check the oil in my car. Then I need to get some cash."

Lists like this work fine—for you. But these words would not mean much to others. For that, you need sentences.

Why Write Sentences?

You may be thinking, "Why do I need to write sentences when I can just stop a pal in the hall, or pick up the phone?" But there is a good reason to write sentences—sentences get things done!

Check each thing below you have needed or wanted to do at one time or another.

    ____ send an e-mail
    ____ let your dad or mom know where you went and when you'll be back
    ____ tell someone where you live and how to get there
    ____ tell why you want a job
    ____ write a fan letter
    ____ tell what **really** happened

Many of these things are best done in writing. Some, like sending e-mail, can only be done in writing. Yes, it's work to write sentences. But good sentences can save you a lot of work—and trouble—by making things clear! In Chapter 1, you will learn about sentences.

LESSON 1   A Sentence Has Two Parts

Who or What?

1. What if a person came up to you and said, "Has a new car." What would you most likely ask that person in return?

___ What is new?

___ Can you drive?

___ Who has a new car?

"Has a new car" is not a sentence. It tells what happened—some lucky person got a new car. It does not tell who got the car.

Every sentence needs a naming part that tells who or what the sentence is about.

Pick the words in the box that could make the statement into a sentence that makes sense. Write the words on the line.

Ted Diamond	Needs some gas	My pet fish

2. _____ has a new car.

Way to go, Ted!

Now finish these sentences. Pick words from the box that will make each statement into a sentence that makes sense. Write the word or words on the lines.

My mom	Fish	The bench	Most people

3. _____ sleep under water.

4. _____ baked a lemon cake.

5. _____ lost one of its legs.

6. _____ like candy.

What Happened?

7. Imagine someone else comes up to you and says, "My pet fish." What would you most likely ask?

___ What did it do?   ___ How big is it?

___ Can it drive?

"My pet fish" is not a sentence. It tells who or what—a fish. It does not tell what the fish did or what happened.

> **Every sentence needs a part that tells what happened.**

Pick the words that could make the statement into a sentence that makes sense. Write the words on the line.

jumped out of the tank	wrote me a note	filled my car with gas

8. My pet fish _____ .

Writing Sentences

Write three sentences about what might have happened when the fish jumped out of the tank. Use some words from the box if you like. (It's okay to use a word twice.)

My pet fish swims in circles all day.

Words for Who or What	Words for What Happened
the fish	did my best
I	ended sadly
this tale	saved its life
	flopped around
	plopped it back in

9. _____

10. _____

11. _____

Sum It Up

12. Check each thing that is true about a sentence.

___ has two parts   ___ can drive   ___ makes sense

LESSON 2   Recognizing Sentences

Try to Find It

One group of words is a sentence. The other is not. Put a check mark by the words that make a sentence.

____ The first one in the water.   ____ Jen will dive from the rock.

Time to Decide

Read each group of words. Write sentence by each sentence. Write no by each group of words that is not a sentence.

1. All the kids and teens. _____

2. The hot sun shines down from the sky. _____

3. Not the best day for a run. _____

4. It is a fine day for a dip in the lake. _____

5. Nick needs to kick his feet. _____

6. The kid with the badge. _____

7. She sees a kid going down. _____

8. In a flash by his side. _____

9. Now she has him safe on the shore. _____

10. Can have fun but must stay safe. _____

KNOW

■ A sentence tells a complete thought.

■ A sentence has a naming part and a part that shows action.

■ A sentence begins with a capital letter.

■ A sentence has an end mark.

Let's Write Some

Draw lines to make sentences. Then write the sentences on the lines below. One has been done for you.

Fred's raft   • are very hot.

He   • has a big leak.

The rocks on the beach   • must swim to shore.

People   • are still coming to swim.

11. Fred's raft has a big leak.

12. He

13. The rocks on the beach

14. People

SPELLING BUILDER

The long **e** sound you hear in **teens** is often spelled **ee**. Can you find three other words on this page that have long **e** spelled **ee**?

LESSON 3 Writing Short Sentences

Two-Word Sentences

You can make up a good sentence with just two words.

Read these two-word sentences. Underline the part that tells who or what. Circle the part that tells what happened.

> **Example**
>
> They <u>skate</u>.

1. Kids run.

2. Planes fly.

3. Cars skid.

4. Max eats.

5. Liz talks.

6. We waved.

GRAMMAR BUILDER

Don't forget to begin each sentence with a capital letter and put an end mark at the end.

Write three two-word sentences of your own. Use some of the words in the box if you like.

dogs	sleep	animals	play	we	snap

7. _____

8. _____

9. _____

Joining Sentences

You can join short sentences using a comma and a joining word, or conjunction. Some conjunctions are and, but, and or.

> **Examples**
>
> Tim snores. Tom does not.   Max eats. Liz talks.
>
> Tim snores, but Tom does not.   Max eats, and Liz talks.

Use and, but, or or to join these pairs of sentences. Put a comma before the conjunction. Write each new sentence on the line.

10. Flags wave. Horns honk.

_____

11. Fish swim. Bats fly.

_____

12. We could take a hike. We could go fishing.

_____

Three- and Four-Word Sentences

You can't say a lot with just two words. So, most sentences have more.

Read these sentences. In each sentence, draw a line under the word that shows action.

Example   The bell <u>rang</u>.

13. I jumped up.   **17.** A kid waved.

14. My dog freaked.   **18.** I know that kid!

15. He yipped like mad.   **19.** He sells candy.

16. I peeked out.

Finish these sentences. Write what might happen next on the lines.

20. I opened _____

_____

21. The kid _____

_____

22. The dog _____

_____

> ### GRAMMAR BUILDER
>
> Use **a** before a word that begins with a consonant sound: **a boy**. Use **an** before a word that begins with a vowel sound: **an animal**.

Write Some Sentences

Try your hand at writing some short sentences. Tell what is happening in each frame.

23. _____

_____

_____

24. _____

_____

_____

25. _____

_____

_____

Go back to the sentences you wrote. Draw a line under the word that shows action in each sentence.

26. Join two of your sentences. Use a conjunction such as **and** or **but**.

_____

_____

_____

Sum It Up

Write letters in the blanks to finish these sentences.

27. A sentence starts with a capital l___ ___ ___ ___r.

28. A sentence ends with an ___n___ ___ ___ ___k.

29. A sentence can have ___w___ words or more.

30. A sentence has to make s___ ___ ___e.

LESSON 4   Subjects

Try to Find It

The part of a sentence that tells who or what is called the **subject**.

Circle the part of the sentence that is the subject.

This car | leaks oil.

Time to Decide

Read each sentence. Draw a line under the complete subject. Circle the simple subject.

1. My car is a pile of junk.

2. It has a big dent in one side.

3. The back seat is ripped and lumpy.

4. Some kid must need a cheap car.

5. I will sell it to the first one with cash.

6. My next car will be so hot!

7. It will zip this way and that way.

8. The seats will not be messed up.

9. My best pals will get the first ride.

10. This job adds bucks to my car fund each week.

Let's Write Some

Make each group of words into a sentence. Write a subject on the line.

11. _____ uses too much gas.

12. _____ should clean out the trunk of his car.

KNOW

■ The **subject** of a sentence tells who or what the sentence is about.

■ The **simple subject** is a noun or pronoun. It names the person or thing the sentence is about. (In the sentence **This car leaks oil,** the simple subject is **car.**)

■ The **complete subject** is made up of the simple subject plus words that help identify the subject.

GRAMMAR BUILDER

The subject of a sentence is usually at the beginning of the sentence.

LESSON 5   Predicates

Try to Find It

The part of a sentence that tells what happened is called the **predicate**.

Circle the part of the sentence that is the predicate.

My cat | sleeps all day.

Time to Decide

Read each sentence. Draw a line under the complete predicate. Circle the simple predicate.

1. The sun sets at the end of the day.

2. My cat rises then.

3. She looks for a handy desk or bed leg.

4. Her feet have spikes in them.

5. Those sharp spikes scratch the leg!

6. My mom yells at her.

7. I get fish out of a flat can.

8. That stuff smells so bad!

9. My dad fills the dish with it.

10. That picky cat eats just a few bites!

Let's Write Some

Make each group of words into a sentence. Write a predicate on the line.

11. Some cats _____.

12. A puppy _____.

LESSON 6   Fixing Fragments and Run-Ons

Fragments

A **fragment** is a sentence that is missing one of its two parts. It could be missing a subject. Or, it could be missing a predicate. Either way, a fragment can be confusing!

Read this paragraph. Draw a line under each sentence that is missing a part.

1–5. Last year I had this odd job. I looked after a pot-bellied pig. This man on my block. Got a pig as a gift. Could not look after it. I had to make lunch for the pig. Cut up a melon. The pig was named Iggy. Just fed him melons and leftovers. How did Iggy get so fat?

Write each fragment on the lines below. Write Who? or What happened? next to the sentence to show which part is missing. One has been done for you.

6. This man on my block _____   What happened?

7. _____   _____

8. _____   _____

9. _____   _____

10. _____   _____

Now fix the fragments. Rewrite each one, and add the missing part. The first two fragments have been fixed for you.

11. This man on my block got a pig as a gift. _____

12. _____

13. _____

14. _____

Read this fragment. Then look at the two different ways it was fixed. Put a check next to the new sentence that is written correctly.

Iggy the pig.

15. ____ Iggy the pig liked hot dogs.

16. ____ Iggy he was a pig that like hot dogs.

Run-Ons

A **run-on** is two complete sentences that have been run together without a conjunction.

Example

Iggy ate the melon he grunted for more.

The first sentence is **Iggy ate the melon.** The second sentence is **He grunted for more.** You can fix this run-on sentence in two ways. You can rewrite it as two sentences. Or, you can join the sentences using a comma and the word **and**.

Fix-it #1: Iggy ate the melon. He grunted for more.

Fix-it #2: Iggy ate the melon, and he grunted for more.

Read this paragraph. Draw a line under the run-on sentences.

17–19. One day Iggy got out. He pushed on his gate he ran into the street. Pigs run quite fast I did not know that. I chased Iggy for quite a while. At last I trapped him he squealed!

Now fix the run-on sentences. You can rewrite them as two sentences, or you can join them using a comma and a conjunction.

20. _____

21. _____

22. _____

Iggy the pig loves watermelon.

Rewrite this run-on sentence. First write it as two sentences. Then write it as one sentence using a comma and a joining word.

I got Iggy back to his pen he slept the rest of the day.

Two Sentences

23. _____

24. _____

One Sentence

25. _____

Spotting Fragments and Run-Ons

When you proofread, look out for fragments and run-ons. If you find one, fix it!

Practice by reading these sentences. Write one of the codes on the line after each one.

F = fragment   R/O = run-on   OK = correct as written

26. One day my pal Drew and I. _____

27. We walked past a pet shop. _____

28. Drew pointed to a huge snake. _____

29. Snakes eat live rats did you know that? _____

30. Drew got a king snake as a gift. _____

31. A long, thin snake with beady eyes. _____

32. Fed it three rats a week. _____

33. Snakes bug me they are too creepy! _____

34. I like my dog his food stays put. _____

Now fix each fragment and run-on. Do this on another sheet of paper.

THINK ABOUT IT

How would life be different if people could not communicate ideas through writing? How would people be able to do the important things listed below?

■ keep track of history

■ spread news

■ tell how to use products

■ pass on knowledge

Sum It Up

Write letters in the crossword puzzle to make words.

Across
2. This is a name for two sentences that run together.
5. One way to fix a run-on is to make it into ____ sentences.

Down
1. A sentence missing one of its parts is called this.
3. Use this mark with a conjunction.
4. One way to fix a run-on is to ____ the sentences together.

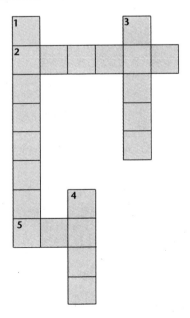

LESSON 7   Four Kinds of Sentences

KNOW

■ A **statement** tells something. It ends with a period.

■ A **question** asks something. It ends with a question mark.

■ An **exclamation** shows surprise or emotion. It ends with an exclamation mark.

■ A **command** tells someone what to do. It ends with a period or an exclamation mark.

WRITING TIP

Many sentences can be written in more than one way.

■ Look out for that rock.

■ Look out for that rock!

■ That is a big snake!

■ That is a big snake.

When writing, you can choose which kind of sentence to write to get the effect you want.

Try to Find It

Put a check mark by the words that tell what this sentence does.

When will the peaches be ripe?
___ asks something   ___ states a fact
___ shows strong feeling   ___ tells someone what to do

Time to Decide

Read each sentence. Write whether it is a statement, a question, an exclamation, or a command.

1. Plant these two trees in the sun.

2. Some plants like the shade.

3. Did you eat any grapes last fall?

4. How sweet they were!

5. This dirt is dark and rich.

6. What a big yard this is!

7. Dig a hole with that spade.

8. There is a big bug on that leaf!

9. The grass needs to be cut.

10. Did you water the beans yet?

Let's Write Some

Read the sentence below. Change it to the kinds of sentences listed.

Bing snagged his hand on a rose thorn.

11. (question) _____

12. (exclamation) _____

LESSON 8   Writing Longer Sentences

Making Sentences Say More

Read these sentences.

    ____ **A** The ape hit its chest and made sounds.
    ____ **B** The big red ape thumped its chest and yelled like a mad beast.

1. Put a check mark by the one that tells more about the ape.

2–3. Which two words in sentence **B** help you picture the ape's size and color?

_____ and _____

4. Which five words in sentence **B** help you understand what kind of sound the ape made?

_____

_____

_____

Making a sentence say more does not mean just adding more words.

Read this sentence.

The ape hit its chest and then it hit its chest again and then the ape let out one yell and then it let out another yell.

5. Rewrite the sentence. Take out the extra words. Change other words so the sentence says more and makes sense.

_____

_____

Now read these sentences.

    ____ **A** We had one dish after another and each one was great and I was stuffed when it was all over and so was my dad.
    ____ **B** My dad and I had duck stuffed with plums, along with a big plate of steaming green beans, and when the meal was over we were stuffed.

6. Put a check mark by the sentence that tells you more.

7. Write a longer sentence about the best meal you have had in a while.

_____

_____

_____

Picking the Right Words

When you write, be picky with words. Try to pick the best words for what you are trying to say.

- **Use specific words.** A word like animal or car does not give a very good picture. The reader may ask, "What kind of animal? What sort of car?"

Read these pairs of words. Circle the word in each pair that gives a better picture.

Example

animal   (king snake)
(roadster)   car

8. meat   ham   10. scream   sound

9. black lab   dog

- **Give details.** Roadster is a better word than car, if you are writing about a roadster. But what does the roadster look like? What does it sound like? Is it new and sleek or old and beat-up?

Read these sentences.

11. Put a check mark by the sentences that give a better picture of the car.

____ **A** The little roadster gleamed like a shiny apple. It gave off a low, mean sound, as if it was filled with thunder.

____ **B** The roadster was stopped at the red light. It sounded okay.

Body Building for Sentences

Make these sentences tell more. Use specific words and add details.

Example

This week I met a girl.

After school on Monday I met a great girl named Lauren.

12. Soon I start a new job.

_____

_____

13. A mean dog came up to us.

_____

_____

14. That DJ is good.

_____

_____

15. Her meal looks odd.

_____

_____

WRITING TIP

When you are asked to write a longer answer, try this:

■ List your ideas on scratch paper first.

■ Work out what you want to say.

■ Then write your answer neatly on the lines where you are supposed to write it.

More Work with Sentences

Pick one of these topics. Write three sentences that will give readers a clear picture of what you are writing about. Use specific words and details.

- a food you like or hate
- a car you would like to have
- the thing you like best, of all the things you have

16–18. _____

_____

_____

_____

_____

Sum It Up

19. Check each thing that can make a sentence say more.
   ___ add specific words
   ___ add details
   ___ just add more words

Just for Fun

Read these sentences. Guess what they are describing. Write your answer on the line.

This is named after a very small animal, but it is not an animal. You move it with one hand. It sits on a pad on a desk. It has no tail, but it looks like it has one.

20. It is a _____.

Part A

Sentences

A sentence has two parts: a **subject** (naming part), and a **predicate** (part that shows action).

A sentence begins with a capital letter and ends with an end mark.

Sentences can be joined using a **conjunction** such as **and, or,** or **but.**

Read each group of words. Write sentence by each sentence. Write no by each group of words that is not a sentence.

1. Vinnie and his pal Jake. _____
2. Got a box of cake mix. _____
3. Vinnie hates nuts. _____
4. Jake got out a pan. _____
5. Will win that prize! _____

Write two short sentences of your own. Use the words in the box, or think of your own words.

Vinnie	cleaned up	mess	the	was	Jake	cake	dropped

6. _____.

7. _____.

There are four kinds of sentences.

A **statement** tells something. It ends with a period.

A **question** asks something. It ends with a question mark.

An **exclamation** shows surprise or emotion. It ends with an exclamation mark.

A **command** tells someone what to do. It ends with a period or an exclamation mark.

Join each pair of sentences. Use one of these conjunctions: and, or, or but.

8. Vinnie yelled. It was too late.

   _____

9. Jake slipped. He dropped the cake.

   _____

10. They will mop up the mess. They will ask Ryan to clean the pan.

    _____

Read each sentence. Write whether it is a statement, a question, a command, or an exclamation.

11. Can you swim? _____
12. I hate the water. _____
13. What is in that lake? _____
14. It was a water snake! _____
15. Get a grip! _____

Read each sentence. Add the right end mark.

16. What in the world is that___

17. It is just an old rag___

18. Well, how did it get here___

19. Do not pick it up___

20. What a nasty thing that is___

Subject and Predicate

Part B

■ The **subject** of a sentence tells who or what the sentence is about.

■ The **simple subject** is a noun or pronoun. It names the person or thing the sentence is about. (In the sentence **This car leaks oil,** the simple subject is car.)

■ The **complete subject** is made up of the simple subject plus other words that identify the subject.

■ The **predicate** is the part of the sentence that tells about the action.

■ The **simple predicate** is the verb that names the action. (In the sentence **My cat sleeps all day,** the simple predicate is **sleeps.**)

■ The **complete predicate** consists of the simple predicate plus other words that tell about the action.

Read each sentence. Draw a line under the complete subject. Circle the simple subject.

1. A little animal walked here.

2. It left its tracks in the sand.

3. A big cat was after it.

4. Those deep tracks go down to the water.

5. Many animals drink there.

Read these sentences. Draw a line under the complete predicate. Circle the simple predicate.

6. The big cat crept up to the cave.

7. It followed the smell of a cub.

8. The mother came out fast!

9. The cat looked at her.

10. It sped away.

TEST TIP

When you take a test, read the directions carefully. Look for words that tell you what to do. The directions for items 11-15 have three parts:

■ Read the sentence.

■ Think about the underlined words.

■ Write an answer.

Read each sentence. If the underlined words make up the subject, write subject on the line. If the underlined words are the predicate, write predicate.

11. The boys set up a ramp. _____

12. They needed a big jump. _____

13. A little kid rode his bike up the ramp. _____

14. His mother could not look. _____

15. The jump went fine. _____

Part C

Fixing Fragments and Run-Ons

Read this paragraph. Draw a line under each sentence that is missing a part.

> Taj needs some cash for lunch. He just has a little bit of change. Rhonda will not lend him any. Needs all her cash for the bus. Taj is in luck. Finds three bucks in his pack! A big sub with ham.

Now fix the fragments you underlined. Rewrite each one, and add the missing part.

1. _____

2. _____

3. _____

Rewrite this run-on sentence. First write it as two sentences. Then write it as one sentence using a comma and a conjunction.

> Taj asked his dad for a ten his dad just gave him a five.

4. Two Sentences _____

   _____

5. One Sentence _____

   _____

Read these sentences. Write one of the codes on the line after each one.

F = fragment   R/O = run-on   OK = correct as written

6. I think Taj needs another job. _____

7. Sells hot dogs at the Weenie Shop. _____

8. He cuts grass he does odd jobs. _____

9. Taj is out of cash again. _____

10. Here he comes hide quickly! _____

Making Sentences Say More

Rewrite each sentence as a longer sentence that says more. Remember to use specific words and to give details.

1. I know a kid who has a pet.

_____

_____

_____

_____

2. One time I saw an animal.

_____

_____

_____

_____

Pick one of these topics. Write three sentences that will give readers a clear picture of what you are writing about. Use specific words and details.

- a fun place to go on a hot day
- a job that bugs you
- a day you look forward to

3–5. _____

_____

_____

Introduction

WRITING TIP

The first sentence of a paragraph should be indented. This means the first word should begin five spaces to the right of the margin. If you are writing on a computer, hit the TAB key to indent.

What Is a Paragraph?

A paragraph is a group of sentences that tell about the same idea. Writers group ideas together to help readers understand what they are saying.

Read these sentences. Put a check mark next to the three sentences that could go in the same paragraph.

_____ A strange animal called a sloth lives in the rain forest.
_____ Some animals look for food at night.
_____ A sleeping sloth looks like a fuzzy gym bag.
_____ Some animals turn snowy white in winter.
_____ Sloths sleep while hanging by their feet in trees.

Stick to the Point

A paragraph can be long or short. The sentences in it can be easy or complex. There is one main thing to remember when you write a paragraph—stick to the point.

Read this paragraph. Cross out two sentences that do not stick to the point.

A sloth spends most of its life hanging upside down in trees.

The sloth is one of the oddest animals in the world. It moves almost as slow as a snail. Its teeth look like pegs. It spends most of its life up in trees, hanging upside down. I get dizzy when I hang upside down. A sloth can eat and sleep while hanging by its feet. In fact, sloths have been known to hang this way even after they have been dead for days. It is sad when a tree dies. If you want to see a sloth, try visiting a South American rain forest. Plenty of sloths live there.

Sum It Up

Check three things that are true about a paragraph.

_____ tells about one idea
_____ can hang from branches after it is dead
_____ has to be very long
_____ helps readers understand writers' ideas
_____ is made up of sentences

In Chapter 2, you will learn about paragraphs.

LESSON 9   Joining Sentences to Make a Paragraph

A Paragraph of Facts

Try your hand at writing a paragraph. Start by writing some sentences about one subject, or **topic**. The picture below shows an ant nest. Study the picture to learn about ant nests.

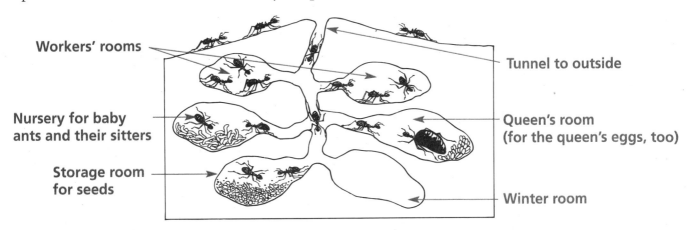

Workers' rooms

Tunnel to outside

Nursery for baby ants and their sitters

Queen's room (for the queen's eggs, too)

Storage room for seeds

Winter room

Write Some Ant Facts

Here are two sentences you could write, based on this picture:

Ants live together in ant nests.

An ant nest has many different rooms.

Write some other ant facts. These questions will help you.

1. Where does the queen live? _____

_____

2. What else would you find in the room with the queen? _____

_____

3. Where do baby ants and their sitters live? _____

_____

4. Where are seeds kept? _____

_____

5. What other rooms are in an ant nest? _____

_____

Remember that
complete sentences

■ have two parts:
a subject (naming
part) and a predicate
(part that shows
action)

■ begin with a capital
letter and end with
an end mark.

Put the Facts Together

Look back at the sentences you read and wrote about ant facts. Make sure every sentence is complete. Then put all the sentences together into one paragraph about ant nests. Write your paragraph on the lines below.

Ant Nest: An Inside View

6. _____

_____

_____

_____

_____

_____

_____

_____

_____

_____

_____

_____

Sum It Up

Your paragraph is almost done—but not quite. You need a sentence that sums up what you have said about ant nests.

Which sentence below would make a good ending? Circle it. Then add it to the end of your paragraph.

- Now you know why ants are such pests.
- I never met an ant I liked.
- Ant nests have different rooms, just as human homes do.
- I like ants.

LESSON 10   Nouns

Try to Find It

Circle the word in bold type that names a place.

Lulu **picks** the reddest paint in the **store**.

KNOW

A **noun** is a word that names a person, place, or thing.

Time to Decide

Circle each word that is a noun.

1. The dresser is old and dull.

2. The girl sands its top.

3. Her dad scrapes the sides.

4. Her mom rubs the knobs.

5. A brush dips into the paint.

6. The first coat is white.

7. The paint dries slowly.

8. Grandpop lifts the lid of the red paint.

9. He brushes paint onto the dresser.

10. The dresser looks so bright!

Let's Write Some

Write a noun from the box to complete each sentence.

mess	sheet	pants	brush	painters

11. You put paint on with a _____.

12. When you paint, put an old _____ down.

13. If you spill paint, it will make a big _____.

14. People who paint homes are called _____.

15. If you sit on wet paint, you will spoil your _____.

16. Imagine that sentences 1–10 were written in the form of a paragraph. Write another sentence that could go in this paragraph.

_____

_____

READING TIP

When the letter **k** comes before the letter **n**, the **k** is silent. The words **knob, knife,** and **know** are examples of this.

LESSON 11   Writing a Topic Sentence

Find the Topic

The subject of a piece of writing is called the **topic**. The topic of the paragraph you wrote in Lesson 9 was ant nests.

Read this paragraph. Think about what its topic is.

> Ants have different jobs. Worker ants go out of the nest to get food. Some ants are baby sitters. They care for the baby ants and stay in the nest most of their lives. Some ants are fighters. It is their job to protect the nest from bugs that want to attack it.

1. The topic of this paragraph is _____. Fill in the circle.

    Ⓐ all kinds of nests

    Ⓑ the jobs ants do

    Ⓒ baby ants

    Ⓓ growing up as an ant

WRITING TIP

A topic sentence is usually the first or the last sentence in a paragraph.

The Topic Sentence

The **topic sentence** is the sentence that tells what a paragraph is about. The topic sentence is sometimes called the **main idea** sentence.

2. Look back at the paragraph about the jobs ants do. Find the topic sentence. Write it here.

    _____

    _____

3. Where does the topic sentence appear in the paragraph? Fill in the circle.

    Ⓐ first sentence

    Ⓑ last sentence

    Ⓒ third sentence

    Ⓓ fifth sentence

Find the Topic Sentence

The paragraph below does not have a topic sentence.

Read the paragraph and think about the main idea.

> Army ants march across the land in big groups. They eat every unlucky bug in their path. Most army ants just feed on bugs and spiders. But some army ants eat bigger animals. Very little is left of an insect after a group of army ants is done with it.

4. Which of these sentences would make a good topic sentence for the paragraph? Fill in the circle.

Ⓐ Ants should not join the army.

Ⓑ Some army ants travel under the ground.

Ⓒ Army ants are hunters.

Ⓓ Army ants march.

The next paragraph is not made up of facts. It is made of **events**.

Read the paragraph. Look for its topic sentence.

> Picture this. It is a warm spring day. A spider has just trapped a fly in its web. The spider stings the fly, and venom makes the fly pass out. Then the spider sucks out the insides of the fly. It is a very bad day for the fly! The spider is feeling happy and lazy. It goes to sleep. It sleeps so soundly it never even hears the army ants. As things turn out, it is also not a good day for the spider. This story shows that a good day for one bug could be a very bad day for another bug.

5. Write the topic sentence here. _____

_____

Read this paragraph. Then answer the questions below.

> Insects have six legs. Spiders have eight legs. The body of an insect has three parts. The body of a spider has two parts. Spiders may look like insects, but they are not.

6. What is the topic of this paragraph? _____

7. Where does the topic sentence appear? _____

_____

_____

Write Your Own Topic Sentence

Read this paragraph of facts.

These harvester ants are working hard.

Harvester ants bring seeds to their nest and put them in store rooms. When the ants get hungry, they bite off the seed husks. Then they chomp on the soft seeds inside. They chomp and chomp until the seeds become mush. The mush is called ant bread. The ants suck the liquid out of the mush. They spit the rest of the seed out.

8. Write a topic sentence for this paragraph on the lines below.

_____

_____

_____

Read this paragraph of events.

The young hiker woke with a start. She scratched one leg, and then she scratched the other. She leaped up out of her sleeping bag. Ants were all over her! She gave out a yell. The yell woke up the leader. The leader saw the ants. She saw the candy wrappers that fell out of the sleeping bag. The young hiker had learned a lesson the hard way.

9. What would be a good topic sentence for this paragraph? Write it here. (Hint—The topic sentence could answer this question: What lesson did the hiker learn?) _____

_____

Sum It Up

10. What is a topic sentence? _____

_____

11. Where in a paragraph does a topic sentence usually appear?

_____

_____

LESSON 12   Common and Proper Nouns

Try to Find It

One noun in bold type names a specific person. Circle it.

Cammie is a **girl** in my class.

Time to Decide

Draw one line under each common noun. Draw two lines under each proper noun.

1. The big test will be on Tuesday.

2. Ed and Luke still must read two books.

3. Those kids go to Gerald Ford High School.

4. Cammie lives in a house on First Street.

5. Sunday is almost over.

6. The light in her room is on.

7. That girl is studying every page!

8. Her mother quizzes her about Africa.

9. Cammie tells her about apes in Uganda.

10. Then she points out a funny picture of a chimp.

Time to Decide More

Draw a line to match each proper noun with a common noun.

11. Mr. Estrada   • place

12. Nashville, Tennessee   • day

13. Easy Freezy Market   • man

14. Saturday   • shop

Let's Write Some

15. What would be a good topic sentence for a paragraph about good study habits? Write it here.

_____

_____

KNOW

- A **common noun** names any person, place, or thing.

- A **proper noun** names a specific person, place, or thing.

- A proper noun begins with a capital letter.

- A **title of address** may be used with a person's name. It begins with a capital letter: Ms. Barbara Cole.

TEST TIP

Who do you think will do better on the Tuesday test, Ed and Luke, or Cammie? Why? Studying for a big test isn't fun, but it's easier if you start early. You also get better results.

LESSON 13   Including Details

Paragraph Facts

Read what you have learned so far about paragraphs.

- A **paragraph** is a group of sentences that tell about the same subject, or **topic**.
- The first sentence in a paragraph is **indented**.
- A **topic sentence** gives the **main idea** of a paragraph.
- A topic sentence is usually the **first** or **last** sentence in a paragraph.

Details, Details, Details

The main idea is the most important idea in a paragraph. **Details** are smaller bits of information that tell more about the main idea.

Read this paragraph. Underline the details that help you picture the morning at Bass Lake.

> Last week I went fishing with my dad. It was just getting light as we pulled up to Bass Lake. The sky was as dark and blue as the water. When I saw frost on the grass, I felt a chill down to my bones. Dad and I got out of the car. We sipped hot mint tea. Steam clouds rose from our mugs and mixed with the smell of pine trees and wet rocks. After a while I warmed up. The first birds started to sing in the trees. Dad gulped the last of his tea. "Time to hit the lake," he said.

Details often appeal to the five senses. Write a detail from the paragraph below each sense.

1. sense of touch   **2.** sense of sound   **3.** sense of smell

_____   _____   _____

_____   _____   _____

4. sense of taste   **5.** sense of sight

_____   _____

_____   _____

6–7. Choose two other details that would fit in this paragraph.
Fill in the circles.

Ⓐ mist on the water   Ⓒ cars honking

Ⓑ red sun going down   Ⓓ insects buzzing

Find Details

The writer of the last paragraph got lucky at Bass Lake. She snagged a yellow perch. Sadly, when she went to write about her catch, she ran out of steam. Here is what she wrote:

I got a fish. It was big, for a perch. It had lots of fins.

You can tell that this writer needs help. The picture below shows a yellow perch. Study the picture and details about the yellow perch.

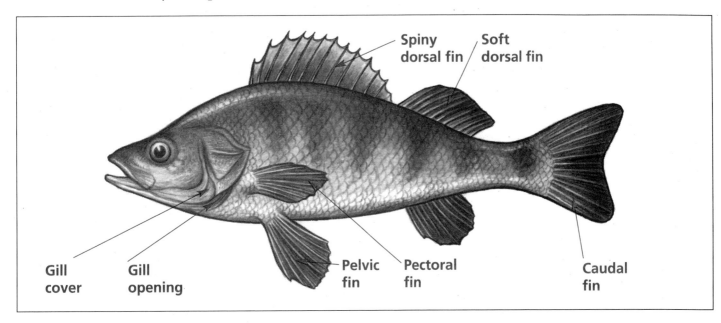

The web below gives some details about the yellow perch. Add other details to the web.

Color: yellow with dark stripes	What it did: flipped, flopped, gasped	Fins: 8. _____ _____ _____ _____

Yellow Perch
Perca flavesceas
5–12 inches long

Size: 9. a big one: _____ 10. a little one: _____	How it felt: slimy, cold, scaly	Shape: 11. _____ _____ _____

Write Details

Imagine you were the lucky person who caught a big yellow perch. On the lines below, write a paragraph describing the fish. Use details from the picture and the web on page 37.

Try to describe your fish so that someone who has never seen a yellow perch can picture it. Answer these questions:

- What color was the fish?
- How big was it?
- What did it do when you pulled it out of the water?
- What were the fins like?
- What shape was it?
- How did it feel when you held it?

12. I caught a big fish! _____

_____

_____

_____

_____

_____

_____

_____

Sum It Up

Imagine that you must tell another person how to write a paragraph that is full of good details. Finish these tips.

Details and Why You Need Them

13. Details are _____

_____

14. Details often appeal to _____

_____

15. A paragraph without any details is _____

_____

LESSON 14   Singular and Plural Nouns

Try to Find It

One of the boldfaced nouns names more than one animal. Circle it.

Kent put two **goats** and a **pig** into the barn.

Time to Decide

Circle each noun below that is plural.

1. animal
2. sentences
3. world
4. hand

5. letters
6. men
7. wishes

8. number
9. day
10. plums

Time to Decide More

Circle the correct plural in each pair.

11. scratchs/scratches
12. mothers/motheres
13. foxs/foxes

14. wolfs/wolves
15. smiles/smilees
16. pianos/pianoes

17. pennys/pennies
18. tomatos/tomatoes

Let's Write Some

Write the plural form of each noun on the line.

19. knob _____
20. toss _____
21. patch _____
22. potato _____

23. life _____
24. berry _____
25. woman _____
26. video _____

27. valley _____
28. mix _____
29. echo _____
30. church _____

31. Write two sentences that describe your favorite berry. Include details that help readers picture its color, size, shape, and taste.

_____

_____

KNOW

■ A **singular noun** names one thing.

■ A **plural noun** names more than one thing.

■ Add s to most nouns to make them plural.

■ Add es to nouns that end in s, x, z, ch, or sh.

■ For nouns that end in y and have a consonant before the y, change the y to i and add es: **baby/babies**.

■ For some nouns that end in f or fe, change the f to v and add s or es: **leaf/leaves**.

■ The plural of some nouns ending with a consonant and an o is formed by adding es: **hero/heroes**.

■ Some plural nouns change spelling: **woman/women**.

SPELLING BUILDER

There is no hard rule for adding s or es to words that end in a consonant and o. Check a dictionary to find out if you should ad s or es to words like **tomato** and **piano**.

LESSON 15   # Varying Sentences Within a Paragraph

Different Kinds of Sentences

Do you like variety? Most people do, especially when they read. That's why good writers use different kinds of sentences.

Read the sentences below. Draw a line from each sentence to the words on the right that tell what kind of sentence it is.

1. Camp was great.

2. We slept in tepees, and we made our own meals.

3. Have you ever picked your dinner from a garden?

4. What huge radishes those are!

5. Never, ever eat a rotten bean.

- question
- command
- exclamation
- two sentences joined together
- a very short sentence

Rewrite Sentences

Write each sentence below in a different way. The words in bold type will tell you how.

6. **Rewrite**…I do not know if you have ever milked a cow.

   as a question: _____

7. **Rewrite**…Milking a cow is not as easy as it looks.

   as an exclamation: _____

8. **Rewrite**…You should act relaxed around cows.

   as a command: _____

9. **Rewrite**…You should not squeeze out the milk too hard.

   as a command: _____

10. **Rewrite**…Did you know that one cow can give about four gallons of milk a day?

   as a statement: _____

11. Rewrite…I like milking cows. I am good at it.

as one long sentence:_____

12. Rewrite…It was fun to do farm work for a while, but I was very happy to get home.

as two short sentences: _____

_____

VOCABULARY BUILDER

When you rewrite sentences to make them more interesting, try using synonyms instead of using the same words over and over. For example, **frighten, startle,** and **alarm** are synonyms you could use for **scare**.

Revise a Paragraph

Read this paragraph. Think about the sentences in it.

I like camping. I like cooking out. I enjoy the smell of camp smoke. I think tents are fun to sleep in. Animals do not scare me. I am into night sounds.

13. What is wrong with the sentences in this paragraph?

Ⓐ They are all false.

Ⓑ They are fragments and run-ons.

Ⓒ They are all the same kind.

Ⓓ They do not stick to the topic.

Write the paragraph again. Try to include a variety of sentence types: question, statement, exclamation, command. Include some short sentences and some long sentences. The first sentence has been done for you.

14. Have you ever been camping? _____

_____

_____

_____

_____

_____

_____

_____

_____

Write Your Own Paragraph

On the lines below, write a paragraph about something you like to do for fun. Include four different kinds of sentences. Include short sentences and long sentences.

15. Title: _____

16. Topic Sentence: _____

_____

17–19. Details: _____

_____

_____

_____

_____

_____

_____

20. Closing Sentence: _____

_____

_____

Sum It Up

Fill in the missing letters to answer the question.

What kinds of sentences should you try to put in a paragraph?

21. d __ f f __ r __ __ t kinds

22. __ x c l __ __ __ __ __ __ s [!]

23. s t __ __ __ m __ n t s [.]

24. q u __ s t __ __ __ s [?]

25. s h __ __ __ sentences and __ __ n g sentences

LESSON 16   Possessive Nouns

Try to Find It

One noun in this sentence shows that something belongs to someone. Circle it.

>   Rick hasn't given Bob's note to Sue yet.

Time to Decide

Circle each possessive noun in the sentences below.

1. None of the kids' phones are working.

2. Sue is in Rick's math class, but she wasn't there on Tuesday.

3. Bob wants to use Sue's sister's car for a road trip.

Let's Write Some

Write the possessive form of each noun.

4. Karl _____   8. churches _____

5. brothers _____   9. plates _____

6. store _____   10. boxes _____

7. Mrs. Chang _____   11. Jess _____

Let's Write More

Write a possessive phrase for each group of words.

Example	the seat of the bike _the bike's seat_

12. the room for teachers _____

13. the waves in the North Sea _____

14. the big house that belongs to Billy _____

KNOW

- A **possessive noun** shows that something or someone belongs to, is related to, or is associated with something or someone.

- To make the possessive form of nouns,
  —add 's to most nouns.
  —just add an apostrophe (') if the plural ends in s.
  —add 's if a plural noun ends in a letter other than s.

Part A   Paragraphs

- A **paragraph** is a group of sentences that tell about the same idea, or **topic**.

- The first sentence in a paragraph is **indented**.

- The **topic sentence** is the sentence that tells what a paragraph is about.

- The topic sentence is usually the **first** or the **last** sentence in a paragraph.

Read this paragraph. Answer questions 1 and 2.

Some planes can fly faster than the speed of sound. The Bell X-1 rocket plane was the first plane to go faster than the speed of sound. The Bell X-1 made this flight in 1947. At first, super-fast jets were used only by the army. In 1976 a super-fast jet called the Concorde was made. The Concorde was the first jet made just to carry people. In the years to come, planes will go even faster. Space planes powered by rockets may fly at 15 times the speed of sound!

1. What is the topic of this paragraph? Fill in the circle.
   Ⓐ the Concorde
   Ⓑ sound waves
   Ⓒ the Bell X-1 rocket plane
   Ⓓ superfast planes

2. Find and underline the paragraph's topic sentence.

Read this paragraph. Answer questions 3–6.

If you travel by train, no one has to drive. People can look out the windows, read, or even sleep. New York is a fine place to visit. Visiting the meal car for a snack is fun. Chips and clam dip make a good snack. Many trains have a car with a glass dome on top. You can sit in the big swivel chairs and watch the world go by. Some trains even have a game room. Taking a trip by train is fun and easy.

3. What is the topic of the paragraph? _____

4–5. Cross out the two sentences that do not stick to the topic.

6. Underline the paragraph's topic sentence.

Read this paragraph. Think about the main idea. Answer question 7.

The chimp is one kind of ape. Chimps live in trees and on the ground. The gibbon is another kind of ape. Gibbons are smaller than chimps, but they have longer arms. The biggest ape is the gorilla. A male gorilla can grow to almost six feet tall.

7. Which sentence would make a good topic sentence for the paragraph? Fill in the circle.

Ⓐ All apes have longer arms than legs.

Ⓑ Many chimps have appeared in movies.

Ⓒ This paragraph is about apes.

Ⓓ Apes come in many different sizes.

Common and Proper Nouns

Part B

Circle each word that is a noun.

1. Risa planted sunflowers in her garden.

2. Six tall plants have flowers.

3. Each flower has many tiny seeds.

4. Mr. Lewis will dry the seeds.

5. Seeds from a pumpkin also make a tasty snack.

Draw one line under each common noun. Draw two lines under each proper noun.

6. These seeds come from Iowa.

7. Ed ordered them from a catalog.

8. That shop is called The Green Stop.

9. Some parts of Alaska have hot weather in the summer.

10. Fog keeps the coast of Oregon cool in July.

Draw a line to match each proper noun with a common noun you could use in place of it.

11. Mrs. Liu	• day
12. Florida	• school
13. Friday	• man
14. Mr. Alvarez	• woman
15. Everett Middle School	• state

■ A **noun** is a word that names a person, place, or thing.

■ A **common noun** names any person, place, or thing.

■ A **proper noun** names a specific person, place, or thing. A proper noun begins with a capital letter.

■ A **title of address** may be used with a person's name. It begins with a capital letter: Ms. Barbara Cole.

Part C   Including Details and Varying Sentences in Paragraphs

- A good paragraph includes plenty of details. Details tell more about the main idea.

- Details often appeal to the five senses.

- A good paragraph includes different kinds of sentences. It has a mix of long and short sentences. It may include statements, questions, commands, and exclamations.

Read this paragraph. Think about details.

A closet can be a scary place. I had not really looked in my closet for weeks. Then I had to find my I.D. card. I was faced with a three-foot pile of stuff. I dug through a layer of stiff, crusty socks. I found food wrappers sticky with oil. I found a candy bar that tasted like the soap it was lying next to. There was also a white shirt caked with mud. It smelled like a play yard. At last I found my I.D. card. Lucky for me, it has a plastic coating.

Write a detail from the paragraph next to each sense.

1. touch _____   3. sight _____

2. smell _____   4. taste _____

5–6. Choose two other details that would fit in this paragraph. Fill in the circles.

Ⓐ dirty jeans   Ⓒ a stove and a sink

Ⓑ a thunderstorm   Ⓓ an old pack of mints

TEST TIP

Many tests ask you to choose one or two answers from a list. Read all the choices before you make your choice.

Rewrite this paragraph on the lines below. Use three different kinds of sentences.

Jamal wanted a cat. He went to the SPCA. He looked at the cats. He was shocked. The cats lived in condos. Each cat had its own futon. The cats were watching TV. The animal workers had turned on a show about birds.

7–10. _____

_____

_____

_____

_____

Singular, Plural, and Possessive Nouns

Part D

- A **singular noun** names one thing. A **plural noun** names more than one thing.
- Add **s** to most nouns to make them plural. Add **es** to nouns that end in **s, x, z, ch,** or **sh**.
- Some plural nouns change in other ways:

leaf	leaves	(change **f** or **fe** to **v**)
hero	heroes	(add **es** to some nouns that end in a consonant and **o**)
baby	babies	(change **y** to **i**)
woman	women	(change spelling)

Circle each plural noun.

1. peaches
2. men
3. mess
4. candies
5. magnet
6. wolves

Write the plural form of each noun below.

7. tomato _____
8. shelf _____
9. bunch _____
10. prince _____
11. lady _____
12. child _____

Circle each possessive noun in the sentences.

13. Take a look at Tiff's photos.
14. She got a shot of all the dancers' moves!
15. This show's cast includes some big stars.
16. It is every dancer's dream to be in a show like this.

Write a possessive phrase for each group of words.

17. the feet of the dancers _____
18. the ending of the show _____
19. the pictures of the students _____
20. the wishes of the girl _____

- A **possessive noun** shows that something belongs to, is related to, or is associated with something or someone.
- To make the possessive form of nouns,
  - add **'s** to most nouns.
  - just add an apostrophe (') if the plural ends in **s**.

Introduction

In the Real World

Getting your point across in writing helps you do well on papers and tests in school, of course. But being a clear writer will help you in the real world, too. Here are just a few of the places and times when writing skills will come in handy.

Getting a Job

- **A résumé:** You can make yourself look good! A well-written résumé will show your talents and work experience in the best possible light.

- **A job application:** How you fill out a job application says a lot about you. It can mean the difference between landing a job and not even being considered.

On the Job

- **Notes and explanations:** You may need to write a note to another worker explaining how and why something happened. You may also need to write to your boss about it. You'll want to make sure your explanation is clear!

- **Business letters:** You may need to write a letter to someone in another company. There is a right way to do this.

Among Friends

- **Friendly letters, e-mails, notes:** Sharing thoughts and making plans together are a big part of having friends and being there for them.

In Chapter 3, you will learn how to write for these and other real-life purposes.

LESSON 17   Writing to Tell What Happened

The Accident

Imagine this. You are on your way home from school. You stop at the four-way stop sign at Crown and B streets. You look both ways. A red car is coming down the cross street to your right. "He will have to stop, too," you think. You go forward.

You do not think about that car again until you hear a CRASH! The red car has smashed into the back end of your car! You get out of the car. The other driver does, too. Both of you are mad. "You ran the stop sign!" you say.

"What do you mean, me?" he says.

Your Side of the Story

Before long a police officer arrives. She asks you and the other driver to write down what happened in a statement. Here is what you write:

Answer these questions.

> **TRAFFIC REPORT**
>
> This tomato head crashed into me. I was driving along B Street. I stopped and he didn't. Now the back end of my car is trashed. Look at my bumper! What a jerk.

1. What important details are missing from this report? Fill in two circles.

   Ⓐ the streets both drivers were on, and the direction each was going in

   Ⓑ the year the other car was made

   Ⓒ a clear telling of events, in time order

   Ⓓ how the other driver was dressed

2. What should the report probably **not** have included? Fill in two circles.

   Ⓐ the command "Look at my bumper!"

   Ⓑ the fact that you stopped but he didn't

   Ⓒ the name of the street you were on

   Ⓓ the words **tomato head** and **jerk**

Help Arrives

Just then your English teacher happens to drive by the site of the crash. She stops when she sees you and your car with the wrecked bumper. You show her what you wrote. She frowns.

List three things your teacher most likely tells you to do when you rewrite your explanation.

3. _____

4. _____

5. _____

A Second Chance to Explain

Now rewrite the explanation. Before you begin, reread the two paragraphs under the heading The Accident on page 49. Pay careful attention to what happened.

6. When: _____

7. Where: _____

8. What happened: _____

9. Why it happened: _____

Sum It Up

Read this list. Write each item below in the chart where it belongs.

10. a lot of feelings

11. what happened

12. name calling

13. when and where it happened

14. useless details

15. how and why it happened

A Good Explanation of an Event…	
Includes	Does **not** include
_____	_____
_____	_____
_____	_____

LESSON 18   Verbs

Try to Find It

One of the words in bold type names an action. Circle it.

Bob and his dad **climb** high **mountains**.

Time to Decide

Draw a line under the verb in each sentence.

1. Bob and his dad plan a big climb each spring.

2. They look at maps and books.

3. Writers tell all about the trails.

4. The two hikers tried Mount Washington last year.

5. Strong winds blow on that lofty peak.

6. Bob reached the summit first.

7. Bob's dad picked the spot for this year's hike.

8. He and Bob have Mount Whitney in their sights.

9. That mountain stands above all others in the lower 48.

10. Their great trek starts at dawn tomorrow.

Let's Write Some

Write a verb from the box on each line.

applies	stay	snaps	carry

11. Smart hikers _____ plenty of water.

12. Each person _____ sun screen.

13. Bob and his dad _____ on the trail.

14. Bob _____ photos at each stop.

Think back to the traffic report you wrote in Lesson 17. Which verb in the box below best fits the next sentence?

smiled	stopped	slowed

15. I _____ at the stop sign on B Street.

KNOW

■ A verb tells what a person or thing does, or helps tell what a person or thing is like.

■ Each sentence has at least one verb.

■ The verb in the sentence usually comes after the person or thing it tells about.

READING TIP

If you come to a word and do not know its meaning, try thinking about related words. You may not know what **lofty** means. But you might know that a **loft** is an open space under a roof or a big space at the top of a building. This can help you figure out that **lofty** means "very high."

LESSON 19   Writing Directions

Why Write Directions?

"How do you make this fudge cake?"
"How do I get to your house?"
"I don't mind taking care of your boa constrictor. But what do I feed it?"

At some time in your life, people may ask you questions like these. When they do, it's useful to know how to write directions.

Directions for How to Make Something
- Include a list of what is needed.
- Write the steps in order.
- Give your instructions in short, simple sentences.

A **recipe** is a set of directions for cooking something.

Read the recipe. Then answer the questions below.

Cheesy Scrambled Eggs (for two)

4 eggs   salt and black pepper
1 T butter or olive oil   1 t hot sauce
$\frac{1}{4}$ cup grated cheese (sharp cheddar)

First heat the butter in a frying pan. Then crack the 4 eggs into a mixing bowl. Beat them with a fork until they are fluffy. Stir in the cheese. Once the butter is melted, put the egg mix into the pan. Add the salt and pepper. Cook until the eggs are firm. Stir the mix to keep the eggs from sticking to the pan. When the eggs are done, eat them right away.

1. Look at the sentences that tell how to make the eggs. Circle any words that tell about when the steps should be done.

2. How much hot sauce do you need? (Hint: Look at the Reading Tip.) Fill in the circle.

   Ⓐ one teaspoon
   Ⓑ $\frac{1}{4}$ cup
   Ⓒ one tablespoon
   Ⓓ enough to fill 4 eggs

3. When should you put the egg mix into the pan? Fill in the circle.

Ⓐ when the eggs are firm   Ⓒ after the butter is melted

Ⓑ after adding salt and pepper   Ⓓ while mixing in the cheese

Write Directions for How to Make Something

Think of an easy meal or snack you know how to make. On the lines below, write directions for making it.

4–6. Ingredients: _____

_____

_____

_____

7–10. Steps: _____

_____

_____

_____

_____

_____

_____

Directions for How to Get Somewhere
- Make sure you know where the user of the directions is coming from.
- Use short, simple sentences.
- Use direction words such as **north, south, east, west, right,** and **left.**
- Include **landmarks**—things that are easy to notice—as a guide.

Read these directions.

First, walk north up Pine Street. Next, turn right at Howard Street and walk two blocks east. Then turn left on Duke Street. Continue until you see County Bank, a big white marble tower, on the corner of Dame and Duke streets. The hotel is on Duke Street across from the bank.

11. Look at the map on the next page. Use a pencil to trace the path from the train station to the hotel. Mark an **X** where you think the hotel is.

> **WRITING TIP**
>
> When you write directions, use signal words like **first, next,** and **last** to signal when the steps should be done.

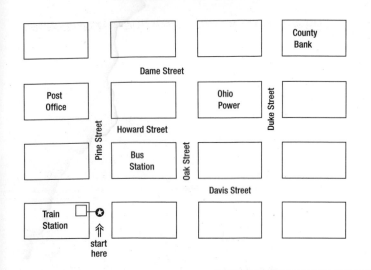

12. Which item in the directions is a **landmark**? Fill in the circle.

Ⓐ the starting point   Ⓒ County Bank

Ⓑ Ohio Power   Ⓓ Howard Street

13. When you turn right onto Howard Street, which compass direction are you traveling? Fill in the circle.

Ⓐ north   Ⓒ east

Ⓑ south   Ⓓ west

Write Directions for How to Get Somewhere

The directions below are supposed to tell how to get from the playground to the school. But do they? Read the directions to find out.

From the playground at 3rd Street, go north on Grove Street. Turn right and then take the first left. You're there!

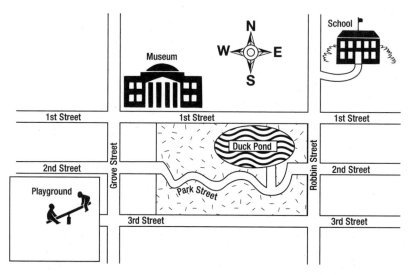

14. Look at the map. If you followed these directions, where would you end up?

_____

15–20. Rewrite the directions so that they tell how to get from the playground to the school. (There are three different ways to get there.)

_____

_____

_____

_____

LESSON 20   Action Verbs

Try to Find It

Circle the sentence that tells about an action.

Bela studies math at City College.   His classes are all in the morning.

Time to Decide

Circle each action verb. Some sentences do not have an action verb.

1. Bela does homework every afternoon.
2. He goes to work about 4 o'clock.
3. Students need money for books, food, gas, and rent.
4. Bela drives a cab for Tuckahoe Taxi Co.
5. A voice gives Bela an address.
6. The address is about ten blocks away.
7. Bela zooms down Kennedy Drive.
8. Two ladies stand outside the house.
9. They are in a big hurry.
10. Bela gets them to the beauty parlor on time.

Let's Write Some

Write an action word from the box to complete each sentence.

whistle	scream	rumbles

11. Thunder _____ loudly.
12. Winter winds _____ through the trees.
13. The sirens on fire trucks _____ shrilly.

Let's Write Some More

Example   Move the eggs while they cook.   stir

Replace each action verb in the directions below with a better action verb from the box.

sprinkle	turn	beat

14. Go left onto Beal Street. _____
15. Hit the eggs until they are fluffy. _____
16. Put salt onto the eggs. _____

LESSON 21   Writing to Give Information About Yourself

Forms Everywhere

People fill out forms all the time. There are forms to fill out for school, for jobs, and for loans, just to name a few.

> **Directions for Filling Out Forms**
> - Print neatly.
> - Make sure the facts you give are right.
> - Use correct spelling.
> - Read over what you have written to make sure it is correct and complete.

Read and Check a Form

The person who filled out this form made three mistakes. Try to find them.

> **Employment Application Form**
>
> Name: Kevin   Bernard   Smith
>   (LAST)   (FIRST)   (M.I.)
>
> Address: 333   Oak Steet   Apt. 5
>   (#)   (STREET)   (APT. #)
>
>   Chicago   IL   60601
>   (CITY)   (STATE)   (ZIP CODE)
>
> If under 18, please list age: __17__
> How many hours can you work weekly? _____ HOURS
> Employment desired   __ FULL-TIME   __ PART-TIME

1. What mistake can you find in the first line Kevin filled out? On the line below, show how he should have written his name.

   _____
        (LAST)   (FIRST)   (M.I.)

2. Circle the spelling mistake in the second line. Rewrite this word correctly.

   _____

3. What part of the form did Kevin forget to fill in? Fill in the circle.
   - Ⓐ his mother's maiden name
   - Ⓒ his age
   - Ⓑ the city and state where he lives
   - Ⓓ the hours he wants to work

4. Let's say Kevin wants to work 25 hours a week. Fill in the two places where information about how much he can work should go.

Fill Out a Job Application

When you try out for a job, you may have to fill out a form like this one. Fill in the blanks with facts about yourself.

THINK ABOUT IT

Job applications often ask you to give **references**. A reference is a person who knows you well, usually a teacher or an ex-boss. An employer may call a reference to find out what kind of worker you are. If you had to give three references on a job application, whose names would you list? Why? What would those people say about you?

Employment Application Form

5. Name:_____
     (LAST)   (FIRST)   (M.I.)

6. Address:_____
     (#)   (STREET)   (APT. #)

     _____
     (CITY)   (STATE)   (ZIP CODE)

7. If under 18, please list age: _____

8. How many hours can you work weekly? _____ HOURS

     Employment desired   __ FULL-TIME   __ PART-TIME

9–10. EDUCATION

School Name	City and State	Years Completed

11–12. WORK EXPERIENCE

Company	City and State	Employment Dates	Duties Performed/ Skills Used
		From _____ To _____	
		From _____ To _____	
		From _____ To _____	

PERSONAL REFERENCES (Do not use relatives or former employers)

     Name   Business   Address

1. _____
2. _____
3. _____

Signature of
Applicant _____

Résumés

A résumé tells who you are and what work you have done. People prepare résumés to help them get good jobs.

How to Prepare a Résumé
- Be accurate: Write only what is true about you.
- Be positive: Focus on what you can do instead of what you can't.
- Be brief: Use clear, simple language.
- Be careful: Make sure there are no mistakes!

Read a Résumé

Read this résumé. Then answer the questions below.

Shandra Williams

1090 Madison Street
Blueville, Wisconsin 53000
555-566-6898

Skills	• Experienced at handling and caring for animals
	• Good office skills
	• Dependable and hard-working
Work Experience	*June 1999–present*
	A-1 Animal Hospital: Greeted pets and their owners. Helped care for pets before and after treatment. Answered phones. Sorted mail.
	July 1998–May 1999
	Pet Central: Clerk Handled cash, check, and charge sales. Helped customers find products. Stocked pet supplies.
	1996–1998
	Various customers: Dog Walker Fed, groomed, and walked dogs of different breeds and ages.
Education	*1997–2000*
	Blueville High School, Blueville, Wisconsin
	References given upon request.

---

13. Draw a box around the job seeker's name and address.

14. In what order does the job seeker list the jobs she has done? Check one.

___ newest first, then oldest   ___ oldest first, then newest

15. Circle the first job listed next to **Work Experience**. Check the things below that the job seeker included.

___ name of company   ___ dates worked

___ her job title   ___ her job duties

Write a Résumé

16–20. On a separate sheet of paper, write a résumé for yourself. Use the résumé above as a model, but put in facts that are true about you.

LESSON 22   Linking Verbs

Try to Find It

Look at the verbs in bold type. Circle the one that is a linking verb.

A big storm **was** on the way. Shandra **grabbed** her raincoat.

■ **Linking verbs** do not show action. They link a subject with information about the subject.

Time to Decide

Draw a line under each linking verb. Some sentences do not have a linking verb.

1. The sky was very dark.

2. No buses were in sight.

3. Suddenly a car screeched up to the bus stop.

4. The driver was a friend of Shandra's.

5. She offered Shandra a ride to work.

6. They were on their way in a flash.

7. Shandra was happy about that!

8. An on-time arrival is a good thing.

9. Other workers were not so lucky.

10. They arrived late, wet, and unhappy.

■ The verbs **am**, **is**, **are**, **was**, and **were** can be linking verbs.

■ The verbs **seem**, **become**, and **appear** are other linking verbs.

Let's Write Some

Write a linking verb from the box in each blank.

was	are	became	is	seems

11. Shandra _____ really good with animals.

12. As a kid, Shandra _____ a nut for pets.

13. She _____ most fond of cats.

14. Shandra's bosses _____ proud of her work.

15. Her friend Mark _____ a vet last year.

VOCABULARY BUILDER

Some phrases do not mean exactly what they say. For example, **in a flash** means "very quickly." **A nut for pets** means "liked pets very much." These phrases are called **idioms**.

LESSON 23   Writing Letters and E-mails

There are five parts of a friendly letter:

■ **date** (month, day, year)

■ **greeting** (how you start the letter)

■ **body** (the main part of the letter)

■ **closing** (how you end the letter)

■ **signature** (your name)

People write letters for many reasons. Different kinds of letters have different rules for how to write them.

Friendly Letter

A friendly letter is written to someone you know well, such as a friend or family member.

Read this friendly letter. Then fill in the blanks with the five parts of a letter from the Know box at left.

February 15, 2003   **1.** _____

2. _____   Dear Kenji,

3. _____

It was so cool to see you last weekend. I'm glad you could come visit. The neighborhood hasn't been the same since you moved away. No one can shoot hoops like you. Now I have to play basketball with my kid brother. Playing against him is like taking candy from a baby. I need a challenge! Maybe I'll go out for the team next year. I just wish I could sink free throws the way you do.

Got to go. Write me, OK?

Your friend,

Jamal

4. _____
5. _____

Write a Friendly Letter

On the lines below, write a friendly letter. Tell a friend about something you have done or are thinking of doing.

7. Greeting: _____,   **6.** Date: _____

8. Body: _____

_____

_____

_____

_____

9. Closing: _____,

10. Your Name: _____

Business Letters

Business letters are often written to give or get information. The tone of a business letter is polite and formal.

Read the letter at right. Then answer the questions.

11–12. Compare this letter with the friendly letter on page 60. What does the business letter have that the friendly letter does not have? Fill in two circles.

   Ⓐ the address of the sender   Ⓒ a closing and a signature

   Ⓑ the date the letter was written   Ⓓ the title and address of the person getting the letter

13. Which of these is another good closing for a business letter? Fill in the circle.

   Ⓐ Sincerely   Ⓒ Later, Dude

   Ⓑ Your friend   Ⓓ Love you

> 230 Sacramento Street
> Grand Rapids, MI 49501
> February 15, 2002
>
> Ms. Leticia Taw
> Sales Manager
> Shoe Biz
> 221 Boylston Road
> Springfield, OH 45501
>
> Dear Ms. Taw:
>
>   Please send me a copy of your spring catalog. I saw the catalog on the Shoe Biz Web page.
>
>   Very truly yours,
>   Charlie Turner

Write a Business Letter

The person who wrote the business letter at right does not have a good grip on business letters.

Write the letter again on the lines below.

      14. Writer's Address: _____

                   _____

      15. Date: _____

16. Name: _____

17. Title: _____

18. Business name: _____

19. Business address: _____

   _____

20. Greeting: _____

21. Body: _____

   _____

   _____

   _____

   22. Closing: _____

   23. Your signature: _____

> 1102 Binky Road Cedar, OH
> 45511
> Mr. Barnett Stowe
> Manager
> The Flip Stop Skate Shop
> 222 Grade Street
> San Francisco, CA 94112
>
> Yo!
>
> You need to know this, man. Those skates you sent me are messed up. They are the biggest hunks of junk! You gotta send me my money back. Okay?
>
>   Later, dude—
>   Ben Beech

E-mail

The **e** in **e**-mail stands for **electronic**. To send **e-mail** is to send a message from one computer to another. Here's how.

- You need to be online—connected to the Internet.
- Put the cursor on top of the "mail" icon that appears on your computer screen. Click on the icon.
- Choose "Send a message" from the menu. (The menu might say "New Message" or "Write Mail.")
- Fill in the blank message form that pops up on your screen. It looks something like this:

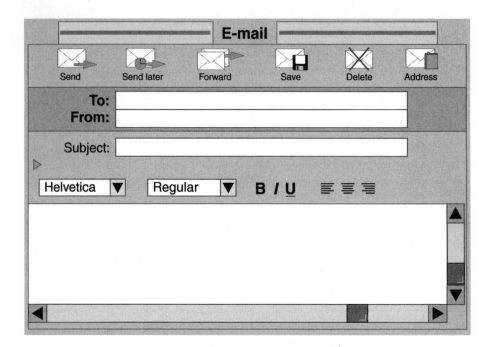

- Fill in the person's e-mail address next to the word **To**.
- Fill in the subject on the line labeled **Subject**.
- Type the body of the message in the big blank space.
- Click on **Send**.

The Power of E-mail

E-mail lets people do many things paper and pencils do not:

- Make an electronic address book.
- Create e-mail groups so you can send the same message to different people at the same time.
- Tell your computer whether to send the message now or later.
- Attach documents, charts, and pictures.

LESSON 24   Writing Dates and Addresses

Try to Find It

Circle each word in the date and address that is capitalized. Then circle each comma.

June 14, 2004
Mrs. Vivian Kazanjian
478 Front St.
Chicago, IL 60613

KNOW

- In an address use capital letters to begin the month, the title of address, the name of the person, the street, and the city.

- Write the state abbreviation with two capital letters.

- Use a comma between the date and the year, and between the city and the state abbreviation.

Time to Decide

Use the date and address above to answer these questions.

1. What is Mrs. Kazanjian's street address? _____

2. What is the two-letter code for Illinois? _____

Let's Write Some

Rewrite each date and address. Use capital letters and commas where they are needed.

3. april 27, 2003 _____

4. mr. pedro aguilar _____

5. 1116 pine ave. _____

6. phoenix az 85012 _____

7. november 4 2006 _____

8. ms. kalisha pender _____

9. 275 conner st. _____

10. oakland ca 94618 _____

Let's Write Some More

Rewrite this address from a business letter. Use capitals and commas where they are needed.

dr. mario p Padrillo
physicians Group west
44 bay st
San Francisco CA 94110

11. _____

12. _____

13. _____

14. _____

SPELLING BUILDER

Proper nouns such as the names of people, cities, and states, can be tricky to spell. Check the spellings of place names in a dictionary. Don't be afraid to ask people what the right spelling of their name is. They will be glad you asked!

Part A — Explanations and Directions

- An explanation of an event includes these parts: what happened; when and where it happened; how and why it happened.

- A good explanation retells events in order.

- An explanation should not include useless details or expressions of feelings about what happened.

This passage tells what happened one day to a boy named Randy. Read the passage and follow the directions.

It was a blistering hot June day. Randy was walking down Bond Street. He had just polished off an ice cream bar. As he turned onto Elk Avenue, he saw a big kid running his way at top speed. The kid was clutching a CD player. As he raced past, he tossed the CD player to Randy. "This is yours now, man!" he said. A few seconds later, two cops came running up to Randy. They spotted the CD player in his hands.

"Got you!" they said as they grabbed Randy by the jacket.

1. Imagine you are Randy. On the lines below, write a paragraph explaining what happened.

_____

_____

_____

_____

_____

_____

_____

_____

WRITING TIP

Writing assignments often ask you to pretend you are someone else and write about what happened to that person. Use the **first-person voice** for assignments like this. This means using the word **I**. The paragraph about Randy's experience might begin with the sentence **I was walking along Bond Street**.

On the lines below, write directions for making a sandwich.

2. Type of Sandwich: _____

3. Ingredients: _____

_____

_____

_____

4–5. Steps:

_____

_____

_____

_____

- Directions for how to make something include a list of ingredients.

- The steps are written in the order they should be done.

- Directions for how to get somewhere include direction words and sometimes landmarks.

- All directions include time-order words, such as **first, next,** and **last.**

Action Verbs and Linking Verbs

Part B

Draw a line under the verb in each sentence.

1. Mitch's dad drives a cab.

2. Sometimes Mitch rides along.

3. One night two clowns asked for a ride.

4. The clowns were smelly!

5. They carried a bag with a big fish inside.

6. The fish was part of their act.

7. Mitch's dad drove fast!

8. The clowns seemed scared.

9. Mitch's dad screeched to a halt at the nightclub.

10. The frightened clowns paid for their ride.

- An **action verb** tells what someone or something does or did.

- A **linking verb** does not show action. It links a subject with information about the subject.

  Some action verbs: **raced, ate, flew, made, sped**

  Some linking verbs: **am, is, are, seem, become**

Draw a line under each action verb. Circle each linking verb.

11. Raj seems glum today.

12. He is very unhappy indeed.

13. He and Sam made a robot.

14. The robot was their term project.

15. They gave the robot six feet.

16. Water jets shot out of its base.

17. It was a rug-cleaning robot.

18. Then a bad thing happened.

19. The robot sprang a leak at school.

20. Soapy water spilled everywhere.

GRAMMER BUILDER

The verb in a sentence usually comes right after the subject.

Part C — Applications, Résumés, and Letters

> ■ **Forms** and **applications** ask you for information about yourself.
>
> ■ **Résumés** tell who you are and what work you have done.
>
> ■ When completing applications and résumés, print neatly. Make sure all the information is complete and correct.

Think about what goes into a résumé as you answer these questions. Fill in the correct circle.

1. What is the first rule of writing a résumé?
   Ⓐ tell what you can't do
   Ⓑ tell the truth about yourself
   Ⓒ don't worry about little mistakes
   Ⓓ say anything that sounds good

2. In a résumé, in what order should you list the jobs you have had?
   Ⓐ from last to first
   Ⓑ from most to least favorite
   Ⓒ from first to last
   Ⓓ in any order

What are three things you should be sure to put in a résumé?

3. _____

4. _____

5. _____

January 30, 2003

Mr. Dale McGraw
Manager
Web Hunters, Inc.

Dude:
   I have this Web site, which is in need of help and I mean big time! I am looking for a Web master. Can you help me?

Later,
Derrick Binder

Read the letter. Then answer each question by filling in the correct circle.

6. What should appear above the date?
   Ⓐ the sender's address
   Ⓑ the address of Web Hunters, Inc.
   Ⓒ the greeting
   Ⓓ a picture of Derrick

7. What is another thing that's missing from the letter?
   Ⓐ the body of the letter
   Ⓑ the address of Web Hunters, Inc.
   Ⓒ Mr. McGraw's job title
   Ⓓ the reason for the letter

8. What is wrong with the tone of the letter?

   Ⓐ It is too formal.

   Ⓑ It needs to be more formal.

   Ⓒ It is not friendly enough.

   Ⓓ Nothing is wrong with it.

■ A **friendly letter** has five parts: a date, greeting, body, closing, and signature. A friendly letter can be light, friendly, and fun in tone.

■ A **business letter** includes your address as well as the address of the business you are writing to. A business letter has a polite, formal tone.

Dates and Adresses

Part D

Rewrite each date and address correctly.

1. november 10 2003 _____

2. mrs. gwendolyn baker _____

3. 4242 green st._____

4. orlando fl 32887 _____

5. october 27 2005 _____

6. dr. Hans baker _____

7. 2711 hyde st. _____

8. evanston il 60203_____

9. mr. ted denton _____

10. april 10 2007 _____

■ In an address use capital letters to begin the month, the title of address, the name of the person, the street, and the city.

■ Write the state abbreviation with two capital letters.

■ Use commas between the date and the year, and between the city and the state abbreviation.

TEST TIP

When you take a test, don't get bogged down! Instead of spending a lot of time on one or two tricky questions, answer all the easy ones. Then go back and tackle the hard ones.

Introduction

- **When** was this poster printed?
- **Why** was this poster made?
- **What** was it trying to accomplish?
- **What happened** as a result of this poster and others like it?

When you study social studies, you ask and answer questions like these. When you write about social studies, you write for these reasons:

1. answer **why, when,** or **how** questions

2. tell the sequence of events

3. give your opinion

4. give facts about a person, place, or event

5. make a judgment about an action or event

Writing well about social studies topics is an important skill in school. Making judgments and thinking clearly about causes and effects will help you in real life, too. In Chapter 4, you will learn how to write about these things.

LESSON 25   Writing About Cause and Effect

Look at the Poster

Let's go back to the poster about fats and explosives. It may not make sense to you at first. But knowing some background facts will help you understand it.

Read this flow chart.

Time: 1943
Place: The United States
What's Happening: America is at war.

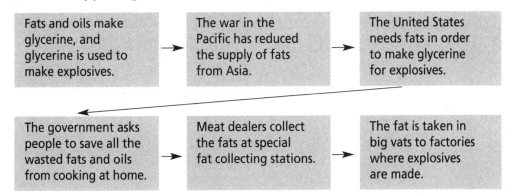

The poster is probably starting to make sense to you. Answer these questions to show what you've figured out. Fill in the correct circle.

1. When was the poster made?

   Ⓐ during World War I

   Ⓑ during World War II

   Ⓒ in 1860

   Ⓓ last year

2. Why was the poster made? Choose two reasons.

   Ⓐ Oil was needed for glycerine.

   Ⓑ Explosives had just been invented.

   Ⓒ The war caused a shortage of oils.

   Ⓓ The war caused a drop in meat sales.

3. What was the poster trying to get Americans to do?

   Ⓐ buy less fatty foods

   Ⓑ make explosives

   Ⓒ join the armed forces

   Ⓓ save cooking oil for explosives

4. What probably happened as a result?

   Ⓐ Americans ate better.

   Ⓑ More explosives were made.

   Ⓒ Meat dealers got very rich.

   Ⓓ Nothing happened.

When you write about history, you can use past tense. Past-tense verbs name an action that happened in the past. Many past-tense verbs end in **ed**. What are some past-tense verbs that **don't** end in **ed**?

Write a Cause-and-Effect Paragraph

Use the facts you learned to write a paragraph explaining why the poster was made and what happened as a result. In your paragraph, answer the questions next to the poster on page 68.

5–8. _____

_____

_____

_____

_____

Revise Sentences

The words **because** and **so** are useful when you write about causes and effects.

> **Example**
>
> The fat supply from Asia was reduced, **so** not as much glycerine could be made.
>
> **Because** the fat supply was reduced, not as much glycerine could be made.

Join these pairs of sentences. Use because or so.

9. Useful fats were wasted during cooking. The government asked Americans to save fats.

   _____

   _____

10. Many basic goods were in short supply. Americans were asked to save or reuse what they could.

    _____

    _____

Revise Your Paragraph

Reread your paragraph. Join some sentences using because or so. Write your revised paragraph on a separate sheet of paper.

LESSON 26   Subject-Verb Agreement

Try to Find It

Circle the sentence whose subject names one person, place, or thing.

Many teenagers stand near the gate.
The big clock says 1:55.

Time to Decide

Draw a line under the correct form of the verb in each sentence.

1. Marina (hold, holds) her music book in her hand.

2. Her friends (wait, waits) behind her.

3. The school band (compete, competes) for prizes.

4. They (travel, travels) to distant cities sometimes.

5. The director (count, counts) the students in the group.

6. The band (have, has) a missing member.

7. The leaders (look, looks) around the gate area.

8. Marina (spot, spots) the flute player at the news stand.

9. The band members (razz, razzes) the wanderer throughout the rest of the trip.

Let's Write Some

Write a verb from the box in each blank.

blow	hand	play	pound
blows	hands	plays	pounds

10. The drummers _____ their drums with vigor.

11. The trumpet soloist _____ a wild series of notes.

12. The flute players _____ a sweet melody.

13. The judge _____ the director a ribbon.

KNOW

■ Verbs that describe present action or state of being have to agree with their subjects.

■ If the subject names one person, place, or thing, then the verb ends in s.

■ If the subject names more than one person, place, or thing, then the verb does not end in s.

LESSON 27 # Writing a Short Report: Planning and Finding Facts

Starting a Short Report

In social studies classes, you are sometimes asked to write a short report. A report gives facts about a person, place, time, or event. Follow these steps when you write a report:

- Pick a good topic.
- Find facts about the topic.
- Organize the facts into an outline.

- Revise the report.
- Write a draft.
- Make a final copy that is clean and correct.

Picking a Good Topic

Let's say you are asked to write a short report about World War II. "That topic is too big!" you groan. You're right. You need to **narrow the topic**. Here's how:

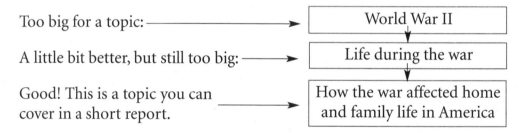

Too big for a topic: ⟶ | World War II

A little bit better, but still too big: ⟶ | Life during the war

Good! This is a topic you can cover in a short report. ⟶ | How the war affected home and family life in America

Finding Facts

You can look for facts in many places:

- library books
- an encyclopedia
- almanacs (statistics and facts)

- history textbooks
- Internet articles
- an atlas (maps)

Use facts from at least two sources. If you can, use both **primary** and **secondary** sources. A primary source is something created by a person who lived through an event. Primary sources include pictures, journals, and newspaper articles. The poster on page 68 is a primary source. Secondary sources are books and articles written after the event was over, by people who weren't there. Most textbooks and library books are secondary sources.

THINK ABOUT IT

When you get facts from the Internet, think carefully about what you read. Ask yourself:

■ Who wrote the article? Has the writer given facts, or just opinions?

■ Can the facts on this Web site be trusted?

■ How often are the facts updated?

Selecting Sources

Read these descriptions of sources.

_____ a 1944 news article about life in America _____

_____ a Web site about World War II airplanes _____

_____ a recipe book published in 1943 _____

_____ an encyclopedia article about World War II_____

_____ a food ad from 1943 _____

_____ a textbook chapter about daily life in the 1940s _____

1. Choose the sources that might have good facts for a report about American home life during wartime. Put a check mark in front of each one.

2–7. After each source above, write **primary** or **secondary**.

Taking Notes

Focus your reading by writing down questions you want to answer in your report. Write each question on an index card. As you read, add notes to the cards. The index cards below are examples of notes you might take.

What kinds of problems did World War II cause for Americans at home?

- Most of the men (18–50 years old) were off fighting—workers in short supply, women and families alone.
- Gas was needed to power tanks and airplanes—gas for cars in short supply.
- Sugar was needed to make explosives—sugar was scarce.
- Metals of all kinds were needed to make ships, tanks, planes, so metal was hard to get.
- Food such as meat was sent overseas for soldiers—Americans back home could not get many foods they wanted.

What special things did people do to help with the war effort? 2

- People drove less. Gas was rationed—people were only allowed to buy small amounts.
- People drove more slowly. Speed limit—35 mph.
- People ate different foods. Sugar, meat, butter were rationed.
- People held scrap drives—collected rubber tires, pots, and pans. These things were reused to make airplanes and tanks.
- Many Americans started growing "victory gardens"—as many as 20 million!
- Women went to work outside the home—shipyards, factories, military bases.
- People collected cooking fats for explosives.

Other interesting details 3

- "Victory Cookbooks"—telling homemakers how to make do with less.
- "Victory Spoons"—for sugar rationing—V-shaped hole made sugar fall through the middle, making people use less.
- 272 million pounds of canned meat were made.
- Many awful recipes for canned meat, like canned meat with pineapple.
- Factory fashions for women—overalls, rags tied around head, work boots.

Let's say you also found the details below. On which index card would you write each one? Write Card 1, Card 2, or Card 3 under each detail.

8. Women served as clerks, mechanics, and cooks at army or navy bases—not combat fighters.

_____

9. Even little kids joined the effort by adding toy cars to the scrap drives.

_____

10. Leather was needed for fighters' boots, so people were allowed to buy only three pairs of shoes a year.

_____

11. Silk was needed to make parachutes, so silk stockings were hard to get.

_____

12. People collected silk scraps and sent them to factories—women gave up silk stockings.

_____

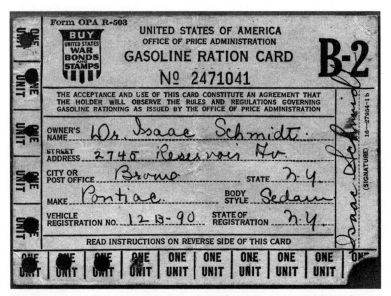

Because gas was rationed, drivers had to carry a card like this one to keep track of how much gas they used.

LESSON 28   Main Verbs and Helping Verbs

KNOW

Try to Find It

The main verb in the following sentence is in bold type. Circle the word that helps it tell about an action.

Lucinda may **paint** a picture of the lake.

■ Main verbs tell the main action that a subject does in a sentence.

■ **Will, can, may, should, could,** and **would** are helping verbs that work with a main verb to bring special meaning to the verb.

■ **Do, does,** and **did** are helping verbs that are used to ask questions and to form negative sentences.

Time to Decide

Draw a line under each main verb. Circle each helping verb.

1. Armando will snap photos of insects.

2. The desert can be very lovely at sunset.

3. A rainstorm could happen at any moment.

4. Did the ranger tell you about flash floods?

5. Dry rivers can fill with water in a few minutes.

6. Hikers should stay on high ground.

7. Lucinda does not do anything foolish.

8. She will finish her painting soon.

9. Do you feel anything?

10. We should wait under the overhang for the end of the cloudburst.

Let's Write Some

Write a helping verb in each blank to complete the sentence.

should	do	will	could

11. Mac _____ lead the way back to the car.

12. Everyone _____ watch for snakes.

13. Lightning _____ strike at any time.

14. _____ you see the car yet?

SPELLING BUILDER

Most compound words, like **sunset** and **rainstorm**, are written as one word. Some compound words, like **flash flood**, are written as two words. If you're not sure whether to use one word or two, check a dictionary.

LESSON 29   Writing a Short Report: First Draft and Revision

Making an Outline

You have found good sources for your report about life in America during World War II. You have taken notes and listed facts. Are you ready to write? Not quite. First you need to make an **outline**. An outline looks like this:

Topic: Life in America During World War II

Subtopic: **I. Problems Caused by the War**
Main Idea: A. Most men had gone away to fight the war.
Details: 1. factories, businesses, farms had lost many of their workers
                          2. women and families left alone

                      B. Many goods were in short supply.
                          1. food (sugar—for explosives, butter, meat—sent overseas)
                          2. gas—needed to power tanks, planes
                          3. metal—needed to make tanks and planes
                          4. silk—needed for parachutes
                          5. rubber—needed for tires
                          6. oil and fat—needed for explosives

II. How Americans at Home Helped with the War Effort
                      A. Women went to work.
                          1. shipyards, factories, farms
                          2. armed forces (drivers, clerks, mechanics)

                      B. People made do with less.
                          1. gas rationing—no driving for fun, 35 mph
                          2. food rationing (butter, meat, sugar)
                          3. 3 pairs of shoes a year
                          4. "victory gardens," "victory cookbooks"

                      C. Things were collected and reused.
                          1. silk stockings—used for parachutes
                          2. rubber tires—for tanks, planes
                          3. scrap metal—used for planes and tanks
                          4. cooking oils collected—used for explosives

1. What kind of ideas are listed next to the letters A, B, and C in the outline? Fill in the circle.
   Ⓐ details   Ⓒ subtopics
   Ⓑ main ideas   Ⓓ topics

2. What kind of ideas are listed next to the numbers 1, 2, 3, and 4 in the outline? Fill in the circle.
   Ⓐ details   Ⓒ subtopics
   Ⓑ main ideas   Ⓓ topics

Writing a First Draft

Write a first draft of the report on the lines below. Follow the outline. Begin a new paragraph with each new main idea. (The main ideas are next to the letters A, B, and C.)

WRITING TIP

A first draft is a first try—a time to get all your ideas down. Don't try to get everything exactly right in your first draft. You will have a chance to go back over your first draft later.

Paragraph 1

3. Main Idea Sentence _____

_____

4. Details _____

_____

Paragraph 2

5. Main Idea Sentence _____

_____

6. Details _____

_____

Paragraph 3

7. Main Idea Sentence _____

_____

8. Details _____

_____

Paragraph 4

9. Main Idea Sentence _____

_____

10. Details _____

_____

Paragraph 5

11. Main Idea Sentence _____

_____

12. Details _____

_____

_____

Adding an Introduction

Your report now includes all the important facts. Is it done? Not yet. It needs an **introduction** that tells readers what it is all about.

13. Which of these sentences might you include in an introduction? Check three.

_____ **A** Between 1941 and 1945, America was fighting in World War II.
_____ **B** People were not allowed to drive their cars just for fun.
_____ **C** The war had many effects on Americans back home.
_____ **D** Everyone had to pitch in to help America win the war.

Adding a Conclusion

Your report also needs a **conclusion**, or a way to sum it up. Without a conclusion, a piece of writing can leave readers hanging.

14. Which of these sentences might you include in a conclusion? Check three.

_____ **A** Both workers and goods were in short supply.
_____ **B** Hardships at home lasted for almost five years.
_____ **C** People got sick of eating canned meat.
_____ **D** By working together, the American people got through the war.

Revising the Report

Read over your report to make it better. Use this checklist to revise your report.

- Does each paragraph have a main idea sentence?
- Are all the sentences complete?
- Can I join any sentences using **because** or **so**?
- Have I used different kinds of sentences?
- Have I spelled each word correctly?

15. Make changes in your report. Check the spelling of words you're not sure of.

Making a Final Copy

On another sheet of paper, make a clean copy of the report. Add an introductory paragraph to the beginning. Add a concluding paragraph to the end. Use sentences on this page for your introduction and conclusion, or write your own.

LESSON 30   Present-Tense and Past-Tense Verbs

Try to Find It

Circle the sentence that tells something about the past.

Rick's aunt and uncle work in a hotel.
He helped them with farm chores last year.

Time to Decide

The verbs in the sentences below are printed in bold type. Draw a line under each verb that tells about something that happens now, or that happens regularly. Circle each verb that tells about something that happened in the past.

1. Many farm family members **work** at other jobs, too.

2. Rick's uncle **does** maintenance for the hotel.

3. Rick's aunt **worked** as a bookkeeper for years.

4. Now she **arranges** conferences and meetings.

5. The two of them **fed** the animals before dawn.

6. Then they **drove** to the hotel together.

7. They **spend** most evenings on chores, too.

8. An energetic teenager **does** a lot in a few short hours.

9. Rick **earned** good money for afternoon work on the farm.

10. Now Rick's sister **spends** her afternoons on the farm.

Let's Write Some

Each sentence below tells about the present. Rewrite each sentence so it tells about the past.

11. Rick attends Kansas State University.

_____

12. His aunt sends him e-mails full of local news.

_____

KNOW

- **Present-tense verbs** name an action that happens now, one that is always true, or one that is repeated.

- **Past-tense verbs** name an action that happened in the past.

- Many past-tense verbs end in **ed**.

READING TIP

Remember that the letter **c** can sometimes stand for the **s** sound, as at the end of the words **maintenance** and **conference**.

LESSON 31

Critical Thinking: Writing an Evaluation

The 55-mile speed limit saved gas and thousands of lives.

Read About a Law

To **evaluate** means to tell what you think and why in a thoughtful way. When you evaluate, you think about what is good and bad about an event or outcome. Then you make your own judgment. This passage tells about a law that was passed in the United States, and how people felt about it. As you read, evaluate the law and its results.

Speed Limits:
How Fast Is Too Fast?

In 1973, there was a gas shortage in the United States. Government leaders found a way to address this problem. The U.S. Congress said it would not give states any money for their roads unless the states lowered the speed limit to 55 miles per hour. Congress did this because the faster a car goes, the more gas it uses.

The leaders knew the law would help stretch the gas supply. They hoped it would have another effect, as well—to keep people safer on America's roads. They knew that the faster people drive, the more car wrecks happen—and the more people die as a result.

The new law did help save gas. It also made the roads safer. In 1974, when the speed law was in effect, 4,000 fewer people died in car wrecks than in 1973.

By the mid-1980s, the gas shortage had ended. Many Americans were tired of the 55-mile speed limit. They felt that getting places faster was more important than saving gas. Even though the lower speed limit had saved lives, they wanted it to end. In 1987 Congress took a vote. They decided to allow states to raise the speed limit on some highways to 65 miles per hour. In 1995, another law was passed. It gave states the right to raise the speed limit even more. Today many states allow cars to drive 70 miles per hour on freeways.

What Do You Think?

Write answers to these questions.

1. Do you think the 55-mile speed limit should have been passed in 1973? Why or why not?

_____

_____

2. Do you think the results of the 55-mile speed limit were good ones? Why or why not?

_____

_____

3. Should Congress have allowed states to raise speed limits after the gas shortage was over? Why?

_____

_____

4. Which is more important to you, getting places faster or saving gas? Why?

_____

_____

5. Which is more important, driving slowly and safely or getting places quickly? Why?

_____

_____

> **VOCABULARY BUILDER**
>
> When you write an evaluation, make your sentences say more. Use specific words and details. Answer these questions as you write. **What** kind of shortage? **How many** people? **How** fast? **Which** law?

Plan Your Evaluation

Use your answers to write an evaluation of the 55-mile-per-hour speed limit law. First, plan what you will say on the lines below.

6. Topic Sentence _____

_____

_____

7. What Was Good _____

_____

_____

8. What Was Bad _____

_____

_____

9. My Own Judgment _____

_____

_____

10. My Reasons _____

_____

_____

11. Concluding Sentence _____

_____

_____

Write a Good Opening

The first sentence of your paragraph should grab your readers' attention. Attention-getting openers include:

- a fact or statistic that makes readers think, "Wow!"
- a quote or saying by a famous person
- a personal story, or **anecdote**, that sheds a special light on your topic

12–13. How could you start your paragraph with a "punch"? Write your ideas here. _____

_____

_____

_____

Write an Evaluation Paragraph

On the lines below, write a paragraph about the 55-mile-per-hour speed limit law. Remember to include a powerful introduction.

14–15. _____

_____

_____

_____

_____

_____

_____

_____

_____

GRAMMAR TIP

Check your sentences to make sure that all the subjects and verbs agree. (Look back at Lesson 26 for help.)

LESSON 32   Pronouns

Try to Find It

Circle the word in the second sentence that takes the place of a person's name.

Luisa takes art classes after school.
She makes carvings out of clay.

Time to Decide

Draw a line under each pronoun.

1. Malcolm invited us to the beach last Saturday.

2. He smiled and waved.

3. I was handed a shovel.

4. Luisa had a paint brush handed to her.

5. Then Malcolm gave us squeeze bottles.

6. They were filled with water.

7. Malcolm led Luisa and me to another part of the beach.

8. It was crowded with people holding little tools.

9. We had been entered in a sand castle contest.

10. Luisa made a sailor and a mermaid, and she got a cool prize.

Let's Write Some

Rewrite each sentence below. Replace the words in bold type with a pronoun.

11. **Steve Rosales** teaches sculpture at Grant Community College.

_____

12. **Cassandra** will take a class from him next quarter.

_____

KNOW

■ **Pronouns** are words that can be used in place of nouns.

■ Subject pronouns (**I, you, we, he, she, it, they**) can take the place of a subject in a sentence.

■ Object pronouns (**me, you, us, him, her, it, them**) can follow a verb in a sentence, or follow words such as **to, for, by,** and **about.**

WRITING TIP

Remember that proper nouns are always capitalized. Proper nouns include names, places, months, and days of the week.

Part A

Writing About Cause and Effect; Writing an Evaluation

Read this flow chart. Then write a cause-effect paragraph on the lines below. Explain how ice cream sundaes came to be. Use because and so in your paragraph.

Long ago, Sunday was a day when fun was not allowed. →	In the 1880s, many towns passed laws against selling ice cream sodas on Sunday. →	Soda fountain owners wanted to get around the law.

Some soda fountain owners left the fizzy water out of the soda. They served ice cream with just the thick, sweet syrup on top. →	They called their treat a "Sunday soda." Today it is called a "sundae."

1–5. _____

_____

_____

_____

_____

_____

_____

_____

Read this passage. On the next page you'll write an evaluation of this strange event.

In 1889, a German ship fired cannons at a tiny village on the island of Samoa. Some American property on the island was wrecked. Angry about the property, America sent three ships to the Samoa harbor. A battle was about to take place. Before any shots were fired, a huge storm came up. Wind and waves sank all the American and German ships. The battle was called off because no one was left in the harbor to fight it.

Write an evaluation of the event above. Answer these questions:

- What was good about the event?   • What was bad about it?
- In the end, was more good done, or was more bad done? Why do you think so?

6–10. _____

_____

_____

_____

_____

_____

SPELLING BUILDER

The words **harbor, baker,** and **solar** all end with the same sounds, but have different spellings. If you're not sure whether to use **er, or,** or **ar,** check a dictionary.

Verbs

Part B

Subject/Verb Agreement

- Verbs that describe present action or states have to agree with their subjects.
- If the subject names one person, place or thing, then the verb ends in **s**.
- If the subject names more than one person, place, or thing, then the verb does not end in **s**.

Main Verbs and Helping Verbs

- Main verbs tell the main action that a subject does in a sentence.
- **Will, can, may, should, could,** and **would** are helping verbs that work with a main verb to bring special meaning to the verb.
- **Do, does,** and **did** are helping verbs that are used to ask questions and to form negative sentences.

Circle the correct form of the verb in each sentence.

1. Huge storms sometimes (hit/hits) the island of Samoa.
2. Waves (crashes/crash) onto the shore.
3. A big wind (rip/rips) trees right out of the ground.
4. People (run/runs) for cover.
5. A tropical storm (last/lasts) for hours or days.

Write a verb from the box in each blank.

help	know	bark	see	close
helps	knows	barks	sees	closes

6. Kimi _____ black clouds piling up in the west.
7. Her two dogs _____ like crazy.
8. Some animals _____ when a big storm is coming.
9. Kimi and her dad _____ all the windows tight.
10. Kimi's brother Kenji _____ them.

Draw a line under each main verb. Circle each helping verb.

11. I will make an outstanding meal.

12. I am planning the menu now.

13. Do you like steak and shrimp?

14. I may grill them on an open fire.

15. Smoke can add great flavors to food.

Write a helping verb in each blank to complete the sentence.

could	will	did	may	does

16. Peter _____ come to dinner, too.

17. He _____ bring a fudge cake.

18. _____ you see Megan on Sunday?

19. _____ she want to join us?

20. I _____ add a place at the table for her.

Present-Tense and Past-Tense Verbs

- **Present-tense verbs** name an action that happens now, one that is always true, or one that is repeated.

- **Past-tense verbs** name an action that happened in the past.

- Many past-tense verbs end in **ed**.

Draw a line under each verb that tells about something that happens now, or that happens regularly. Circle each verb that tells about the past.

21. My friend Justin has the lead role in the play I attended.

22. He plays the part of an old rock star.

23. The star wrecked his voice by screaming out his songs.

24. Now he sells used cars in L.A.

25. Justin performed this sad role with great skill.

Part C

Writing a Short Report

The sentences below tell the steps for writing a short report. The steps are out of order. Write the numbers 1–8 on the lines to show the order in which the steps should be done.

1. ____ Write a first draft.

2. ____ Take notes on index cards.

3. ____ Revise the report to make it better.

4. ____ Pick a good topic.

5. ____ Make a final copy.

6. ____ Make an outline.

7. ____ Find the facts.

8. ____ Select sources.

The short report below has some mistakes in it. Read the report and answer the questions.

      Mount Washington, New Hampshire has some of the worst weather on earth. Two different storm tracks come together over Mount Washington. Cold storms from the North Pole mix with warm storms from the tropics. Winds have reached 231 miles per hour at Mount Washington's summit—the strongest winds ever measured. Death Valley, California is the hottest place in North America. On a summer day, the air can reach 134°F. Ground heat can reach almost 201°F! Death Valley is also one of the driest places in North America. Some years less than $\frac{1}{10}$ of an inch of rain falls there.

9. One thing the writer forgot to do is divide the report into paragraphs. Put this mark in front of the sentence that should begin a new paragraph: ¶

10. The report above is missing a main idea sentence. Choose the sentence that tells what the whole report is about.

    Ⓐ Now you know why they call it Death Valley.

    Ⓑ Two places in North America are weather record-breakers.

    Ⓒ A little bit of wind can clean out your head.

    Ⓓ Death Valley is too hot to visit in summer.

Pronouns

Part D

- **Pronouns** are words that can be used in place of nouns.
- Subject pronouns (**I, you, we, he, she, it, they**) can take the place of a subject in a sentence.
- Object pronouns (**me, you, us, him, her, it, them**) can follow a verb in a sentence, or follow words such as **to, for, by,** and **about**.

TEST TIP

When you take a writing test, carefully look at each test question. What form should your answer be in? Some questions may ask for an essay, some for a paragraph, and others for a sentence or two.

Draw a line under each pronoun.

1. We need to bring plenty of water on the hike.
2. I will bring two canteens.
3. Will you share that water with Jenna and Mike?
4. No, they need to bring water, too.
5. It would be foolish of us to get heatstroke.

Rewrite each sentence. Replace each word in bold type with a pronoun.

6. **Jenna** isn't used to hiking. _____

7. **Kay** will lend a hat to Jenna. _____

8. **Flip-flops** are not good for hiking. _____

9. I asked **Mike** to get Jenna's boots from the trunk. _____

10. Now **Jenna and I** are ready. _____

Introduction

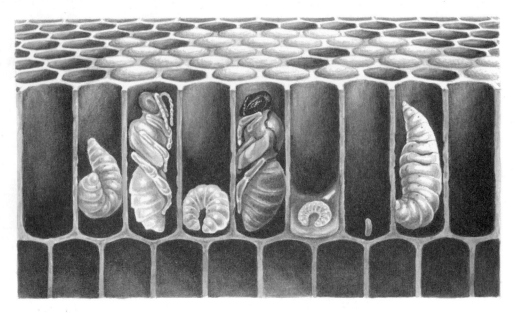

1. Look at these pictures. What do you think they show?

___ insect mummies   ___ a new snack food
___ space aliens   ___ baby bees

2. What do you think the creatures in the picture are doing?

___ dying   ___ growing up
___ sleeping in   ___ finding food

A big part of science is asking questions like these and trying out different ways of answering them. Scientists also write about what they learn. You may be asked to write as a part of your science classes, too. Here are some things you may need to explain when you write about science:

- the steps you followed to find an answer
- the result or outcome of an experiment
- a sequence of events
- the steps in a process
- how something works
- why something happens

In Chapter 5, you will learn to write about science.

LESSON 33   Writing About Sequence

Time Lines

You may be asked to write about how something in the natural world grows or changes. This time line shows events in the life of a worker honeybee.

The Life of a Worker Honeybee

Life Begins — An egg is laid in a wax cell inside the hive. A white worm called a grub hatches from the egg.

Week 1 — The grub eats constantly for about six days. Nurses feed it 1,300 meals of honey and pollen a day. When the grub is big enough to fill the cell, nurses cover the cell with a wax lid, sealing it tight.

Week 2 — The grub changes form inside the cell. Little by little, it becomes a bee. When it is ready, the bee gnaws through the wax cap. In about 12 days the bee comes out of the cell fully grown.

Week 3 — The new bee rests.

Week 4 — **Job #1:** The adult bee's first job inside the hive is feeding the new grubs pollen and honey. This job lasts for about a week.

Week 5

Week 6 — **Job #2:** The bee starts to make wax. It uses the wax to make the hive bigger. It also has other jobs inside the hive. It might take dead bees out of the hive or clean out old cells.

Week 7 — **Job #3:** The bee starts working outside the hive gathering pollen and nectar. It brings these back to the hive for honey.

Week 8

Week 9

Life Ends — The worker bee dies after about six weeks of adult life.

Use a Time Line

Use the time line to answer these questions. Fill in the correct circles.

1. About how long does a bee live, from the time it hatches to the time it dies?

Ⓐ 6 days   Ⓒ 6 weeks

Ⓑ 2 weeks   Ⓓ 9 weeks

Show the order in which each stage of a bee's life happens. Write a number from 1 to 5 on the line next to each item.

2. _____ The bee gathers pollen and nectar.

3. _____ The grub eats 1,300 meals a day.

4. _____ The bee is a nurse for the new grubs.

5. _____ The bee gnaws through the wax seal.

6. _____ The bee uses its own wax to build up the hive.

Write About Bees

On the lines below, write a paragraph about the first three weeks in a honeybee's life. Use facts from the time line. Here are some tips:

- Tell about the events in the order they happen.
- Use sequence words, such as **first, next,** and **then.**
- Give specific time periods, such as **in six days.**

7. Topic Sentence: _____

_____

_____

8. From egg to grub: _____

_____

_____

9. From grub to bee: _____

_____

_____

THINK ABOUT IT

Time lines are useful tools when you are asked to write about sequence. Think about something you know how to do that must happen in sequence. Make a time line showing all steps or stages.

The Bee as an Adult

On another sheet of paper, write two paragraphs about the adult phase of a bee's life. First decide what the topic of each paragraph should be. Circle the two topics that make sense as subjects for the paragraphs. Then write two paragraphs on your paper.

10. Circle two topics for your paragraphs.
- making wax and gathering nectar
- jobs inside the hive and jobs outside the hive
- gnawing through wax and being a nurse
- hatching and dying

LESSON 34   Commas in Lists

Try to Find It

Circle the three things listed in this sentence. Then draw an arrow pointing to each comma.

You can enjoy exciting races, loud concerts, and big-time sporting events at South County Park.

Time to Decide

Add commas where they are needed in each sentence.

1. My sister my aunt and I are all racing fans.

2. Do you like stock cars Indy cars or funny cars best?

3. Drivers must have good eyesight strong hands and steady nerves.

4. The car the driver and the pit crew must all perform flawlessly for success.

5. Races are held at South County Park on Tuesdays Thursdays Saturdays and Sundays during the summer.

6. We bring hats binoculars seat cushions snacks and water.

7. Do you know what the yellow flag the red flag and the checkered flag mean?

8. Nick has raced pickup trucks motorcycles and even tractors.

9. He has won ribbons trophies and cash prizes.

10. His motto is *FSS,* which stands for fast smart and safc.

Let's Write Some

Add a list to complete each sentence. Use commas where they are needed.

11. The best months to take a vacation are _____

    and _____.

12. The most exciting events to attend are _____

    and _____.

- If a sentence contains a list of three or more things, use a comma after each item except the last one.

- The last comma goes before the word **and** or **or**.

LESSON 35   Writing a Research Report, Part 1

Using Different Kinds of Sources

A research report is like a short report, only longer. When you write a research report, you need to find facts from many different sources. Let's say you need to write a research report about volcanoes. Many different kinds of sources can give you information about this topic.

Graphic Aids

Photos, diagrams, and **maps** are called **graphic aids.** Graphic aids give facts using a mix of pictures, numbers, or words. This diagram shows the parts of a volcano.

A Glossary

Many nonfiction books and textbooks have a **glossary** in the back. A glossary gives the meanings of special words used in the book. If you're not sure what a word means, check the glossary. This glossary explains words that have to do with volcanoes.

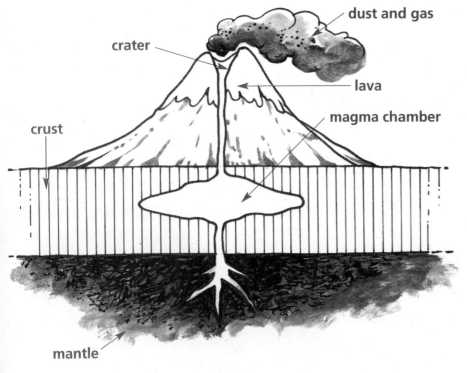

crater a bowl-shaped hole, as in a volcano

crust the outer layer of earth

erupt to explode and throw out lava and hot gas

lava the hot liquid rock that comes out of a volcano

magma hot liquid rock from deep inside the earth

magma chamber a space under the earth where magma forms a pool

main vent the main opening in a volcano, where lava flows out

mantle the layer of earth just below the crust, where most magma forms

side vent a smaller opening in the side of a volcano, where lava flows out

volcano an opening in the earth's surface from which lava, rocks, and hot gases erupt

A Flow Chart

This chart shows how a volcano is formed.

Magma deep inside the earth melts the rock around it. Gas from the melted rock mixes with the magma.	The mix of gas and magma is lighter than the rock around it. The hot magma melts big gaps in the rock, forming a magma chamber.	The gas-filled magma lake blasts a channel through a weakened part of the rock.
The magma mass moves up toward the earth's surface. The gas is released. It blasts a hole through the surface.	Hot rocks and magma erupt through the vent. Lava and rocks pile up around the vent, forming a volcano.	Over time, a crater shaped like a bowl forms at the top of the volcano.

Pictures and Captions

These pictures show the three main kinds of volcanoes. The words under the pictures, or **captions,** explain how each kind is formed.

 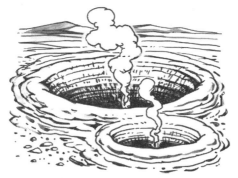 

A **cinder cone** is formed when volcanic rocks erupt and then fall all around the vent. A cinder cone is short and has a flat top.

A **shield volcano** forms when lava erupts from many different vents and then overlaps. The lava spreads out and builds up a low, wide mountain.

Most volcanoes are **composite,** or **cone-shaped**. Lava and hot rocks build up a tall mountain shaped like a cone, with a crater on top.

Making an Outline

Finish the outline by adding facts from pages 92 and 93. Some facts have been filled in for you.

Topic: <u>Volcanoes</u>

I. **How a Volcano Forms**

    A. Magma from deep inside the earth melts the rock around it, making a mix of gas and magma.

    B. _____

    C. _____

    D. _____

    E. _____

    F. _____

II. **Different Kinds of Volcanoes**

    A. Cinder cone

        1. forms when volcanic rocks pile up around the vent

        2. short with a flat top

    B. _____

        1. _____

        2. _____

    C. _____

        1. _____

        2. _____

III. **The Parts of a Volcano**

    A. Deep under the earth

        1. _____

        2. _____

    B. Inside the volcano itself

        1. _____

        2. _____

    C. Outside the volcano

        1. _____

        2. _____

Writing a First Draft

Write a first draft of the research report about volcanoes here. Begin with an introduction that tells what volcanoes are and why people are interested in them. Next, use the outline on page 94 to write the main part of your report. Make each subtopic listed by the numbers I, II, and III into a paragraph. Then write a conclusion telling again how volcanoes can be different, but how they are all similar.

use the outline on page 94

Title: _____

Paragraph 1:
Introduction _____

_____

_____

_____

Paragraph 2: _____

_____

_____

_____

Paragraph 3: _____

_____

_____

_____

Paragraph 4: _____

_____

_____

_____

Paragraph 5:
Conclusion _____

_____

_____

_____

VOCABULARY BUILDER

Many words have more than one form. Examples are: **volcano** and **volcanic; erupt** and **eruption**. Knowing the meaning of one form can help you figure out the meaning of other forms.

LESSON 36 Adjectives

Try to Find It

Circle the two words in bold type that tell about a noun.

> Carmina **strongly** dislikes **the red** carpet in the hall.

Time to Decide

Draw a line under each adjective. Circle each article.

1. Uncle Ernesto loves the soft brown chair.

2. Aunt Irma wants a wooden rocker in that corner.

3. Do we really need a new couch?

4. The old sofa has comfortable seats for four people.

5. The red drapes have ugly spots on them.

6. Grandma has made lovely drapes for those windows.

7. Is an ottoman a stool or a table?

8. A tall, shiny lamp would look nice by the sofa.

9. No, Eddie, we are not getting a giant TV.

10. This room will soon be elegant and functional.

Let's Write Some

Write a or an before each noun.

11. _____ vent

12. _____ ember

13. _____ gas

14. _____ rock

15. _____ volcano

16. _____ eruption

17. _____ channel

18. _____ cinder

19. _____ crater

20. _____ ash

21. _____ effect

22. _____ hour

LESSON 37   Writing a Research Report, Part 2

Revising

When you revise a report, you change parts of it to make it better. Ask yourself these questions when revising a research report:
- Are the ideas grouped into paragraphs?
- Does each paragraph have a topic sentence?
- Have I included an introduction and a conclusion?
- Are all the facts right?
- Are my sentences clearly and correctly written?
- Have I used different kinds of sentences so the report is interesting to read?

Practice Revising

Read this short report. Look for five mistakes. You will fix the mistakes on the lines below the short report.

> Every beehive has a queen the queen is much bigger than the other bees. A bee is not born to be a queen. Rather, a bee becomes a queen by being fed a special diet. While still a grub. The queen-to-be is fed rich food. She grows big and strong. Some worker bees clean the hive. The queen bee is very important to the hive. Only she can lay eggs. The other bees care for the queen all her life. Worker bees do different jobs in the hive. Some stay by the hive's entry and keep other insects away. Others go out into the world and gather nectar. Gather pollen, too. By working hard at their special jobs, all these bees help a beehive prosper.

These are the five mistakes. Fix the mistakes on the lines below.
- The report should be broken into two paragraphs.
- Two sentences are fragments.
- One sentence is a run-on.
- One idea is out of place.

1. Put this mark in front of the sentence that should begin a new paragraph: ¶

2–3. Correct the two fragments.

Fragment #1: _____

_____

Fragment #2: _____

_____

SPELLING BUILDER

When you use a word processor, you can use the spell checker to find misspelled words. But be careful of words you may have misused but spelled correctly. Is it **blue** or **blew**? Proofread even when you use a spell checker!

4. Fix the run-on. _____

_____

5. Underline the sentence that is out of place. Draw an arrow to a place where it could go.

Revise Your Report

Reread the report about volcanoes you wrote in Lesson 35 on page 95.

6. Ask yourself each question on the checklist at the top of page 97. If you answer **no** to any question, make changes in the report.

Proofreading

When you proofread a piece of writing, you read it carefully and fix mistakes. The box below shows the marks proofreaders use to fix mistakes.

Proofreader's Marks

Mark	Meaning	Example
℘	take out	Volcanoes are are scary.
∧	add	Is Mt. Whitny a volcano?
=	use a capital letter	Many volcanoes are in mexico.
/	use a lowercase letter	That lava is Hot!
sp	check spelling	What is a cinder kone volcano? sp

Practice Proofreading

Read this paragraph.

   Mount St. Helens is in the state of washington. In 1980 this ountain blew its top. It erupted on May 18th. Mount St. Heleans spewed out lava, ash, and hot rocks. Trees were knocked down down like matchsticks. Though scientists predicted the eruption, They were shocked by its power.

7–12. Find six mistakes. Use proofreader's marks to fix them.

Proofread Your Report

13. Reread your report about volcanoes carefully. Use proofreader's marks to fix any mistakes you find.

Publishing

To publish a piece of writing is to make a final copy that is neat and correct. You can type a report on a word processor, or you can write it neatly by hand.

14. Make a final copy of your volcano report. If you can, use a word processor.

LESSON 38 Adverbs

Try to Find It

Circle the word that tells how something is done.

The director claps her hands impatiently.

Time to Decide

Draw a line under the adverb in each sentence.

1. A tall man hollers loudly.

2. He walks steadily toward three youths.

3. The camera rotates slowly.

4. One of the youths gestures menacingly.

5. The man suddenly flashes a badge.

6. The youths instantly freeze.

7. "Cut!" yells the director sharply.

8. "We must shoot that again," she says.

9. The actors quickly take their places.

10. Making a movie always takes patience.

Let's Write Some

Write an adverb from the box in each blank.

| enthusiastically | reluctantly | carelessly | rapidly |

11. Our dog goes outside for the night _____.

12. Cynthia has a lot to say, so she speaks _____.

13. Having enjoyed the play, the audience clapped _____.

14. Kevin made a mess because he poured the paint _____.

KNOW

- An **adverb** can describe the action of a verb.

- Adverbs can tell **how, when,** or **where** about an action, or they can give other information.

- Many adverbs are formed by adding **ly** to adjectives. They often tell how; for example, **swiftly, diligently.**

- Some adverbs do not end in **ly.** They often tell when or where; for example, **today, outside.**

READING TIP

Often when the letter **g** begins a word and is followed by the letter **e**, it makes the **j** sound. The word **gestures** begins with the **j** sound.

LESSON 39   Critical Thinking: Writing an Opinion

Think About It

Read each statement below. If you agree with it, circle agree. If you do not agree, circle disagree.

- It's rude to use cell phones in public.   **agree**   **disagree**
- Public school students should not have to   **agree**   **disagree**
  wear uniforms.
- Hand-held games are bad for kids.   **agree**   **disagree**

You have just given your **opinion** about three topics. When you write about your opinions, you need to tell why you feel and think as you do. This passage gives one writer's opinion about hand-held games for kids. As you read, think about where you stand.

Hand-Held Toys: A Dangerous Game

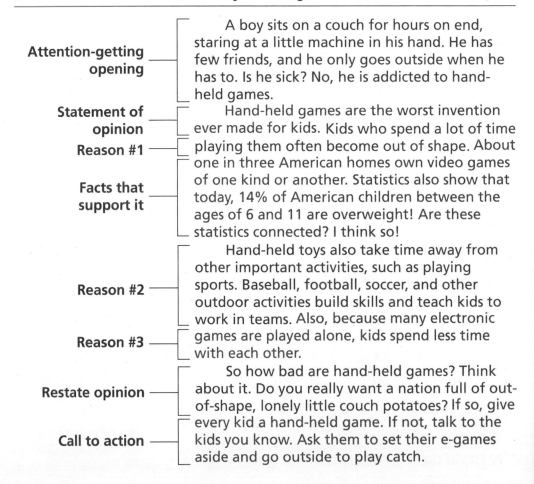

Attention-getting opening —— A boy sits on a couch for hours on end, staring at a little machine in his hand. He has few friends, and he only goes outside when he has to. Is he sick? No, he is addicted to hand-held games.

Statement of opinion —— Hand-held games are the worst invention ever made for kids. Kids who spend a lot of time

Reason #1 —— playing them often become out of shape. About

Facts that support it —— one in three American homes own video games of one kind or another. Statistics also show that today, 14% of American children between the ages of 6 and 11 are overweight! Are these statistics connected? I think so!

Reason #2 —— Hand-held toys also take time away from other important activities, such as playing sports. Baseball, football, soccer, and other outdoor activities build skills and teach kids to work in teams. Also, because many electronic games are played alone, kids spend less time

Reason #3 —— with each other.

Restate opinion —— So how bad are hand-held games? Think about it. Do you really want a nation full of out-of-shape, lonely little couch potatoes? If so, give every kid a hand-held game. If not, talk to the

Call to action —— kids you know. Ask them to set their e-games aside and go outside to play catch.

What Do You Think?

After you read the passage about hand-held games, answer these questions.

1. Draw a line under the sentence that states the writer's opinion. Do you agree with the opinion?

   _____

   _____

2–4. Write the three reasons the writer gives for the opinion.

   Reason #1 _____

   _____

   Reason #2 _____

   _____

   Reason #3 _____

   _____

5. Underline the two facts the writer uses to support reason #1.

Plan an Opinion Essay

Let's say you disagree with the writer about hand-held games. Here's your chance to say it in writing. Make notes on the lines below to help you plan your writing.

6. Attention-getting opening_____

   _____

   _____

7. Statement of opinion _____

   _____

8. Reason #1 _____

   _____

   _____

9. Reason #2 _____

   _____

   _____

In many writing tests you see a **writing prompt** like this one.

■ Look for key words in the prompt that tell you what to do.

■ Plan your response by making an outline.

10. Reason #3 _____

_____

_____

11. Restate opinion _____

_____

_____

12. Call to action _____

_____

_____

Write Your Opinion

On the lines below, write a short essay giving your opinion of hand-held games. Tell whether or not you think they are a good use of young people's time. Make sure you tell why you think as you do.

13–15. _____

_____

_____

_____

_____

_____

_____

_____

_____

_____

_____

_____

_____

_____

_____

LESSON 40   Prepositions

Try to Find It

Read this sentence. Circle the word that tells where around the tree the squirrel ran.

The squirrel skittered beside the oak tree.

Time to Decide

Draw a line under the preposition in each sentence.

1. Rena paints with watercolors.

2. She spends many mornings in the park.

3. The pond beside the botanical garden is a favorite spot.

4. Ducks float on the pond.

5. Frogs leap among the reeds.

6. She catches these creatures on paper.

7. Rena recently retired from her job.

8. She never had much time for art.

9. Now her life revolves around painting.

10. Next month she will display her artwork at the center for elders.

Let's Write Some

Write a preposition from the box in each blank.

over	through	under	inside

11. A deer leaped _____ the fence.

12. A gopher burrowed _____ the wall.

13. Somehow a mouse got _____ our cooler.

14. I shouldn't have walked _____ the mud.

KNOW

■ A **preposition** is a word that relates a noun to another word or phrase in the sentence.

■ A **prepositional phrase** contains at least a preposition and a noun. It may contain other words that modify the noun, such as articles and adjectives.

■ Some common prepositions are **to, in, on, under, of, for, from, across, between,** and **behind**.

VOCABULARY BUILDER

Adding the suffix **al** to certain words can make new words related in meaning. For example, **musical** means "related to music," and **botanical** means "related to botany," which is the study of plants.

Part A   Writing About Sequence; Writing an Opinion

Read this fact sheet about the La Brea Tar Pits.

Fact Sheet: The La Brea Tar Pits

The Time: 1906
The Place: Los Angeles, California

What Happened: The remains of a huge Ice Age bear were found in a sticky bog of tar and oil. People kept digging. Over time, more than a million Ice Age animal skeletons were found. The bog became known as the La Brea Tar Pits.

Why: During the Ice Age, about 10,000 years ago, a huge bog full of tar and oil existed in what is now downtown L.A. A pool of water covered the bog. Animals went to drink at the pool. They became trapped in the sticky tar and died. The tar kept the animals from rotting, so their remains stayed intact.

The Tar Pits Today: The tar pit still exists in downtown L.A. It is much smaller than the Ice Age bog. But even now people have to watch where they step in the area near the bog.

Write a paragraph about the La Brea Tar Pits. Include all the events in the fact sheet, but write about them in the order they happened.

1–5. _____

_____

_____

_____

_____

Read this passage. Think about what your opinion is.

Music and Freedom of Speech

One of the most important rights we have in America is freedom of speech. Freedom of speech is the right to express opinions and beliefs without fear. Are there cases in which people's freedom to say what they want should be limited? Some people say yes. A number of people have said that some rap songs are bad for kids to hear. They want the government to forbid rap songs that seem to support breaking laws or mistreating people. Meanwhile, the writers of the songs say they have the right to express whatever they think and feel. What do you think?

Write a paragraph expressing your opinion. Answer this question: Should freedom of speech ever be limited by the government? Why or why not?

6–10. _____

_____

_____

_____

_____

Commas and Prepositions

Add commas where they are needed in each sentence.

1. The volcano blew out gas ashes and lava.
2. The lava flow covered trees homes rivers and roads.
3. Scientists photographers and firefighters looked on.
4. It was time for birds animals and people to flee.
5. The sky grew gray smoky and full of ash.

■ If a sentence contains a list of three or more things, use a comma after each item except the last one.

■ The last comma goes before the word **and** or **or**.

Add a list of at least three things to complete each sentence. Use commas where they are needed.

6. We put _____ in our survival kit.
7. We saw _____ on the way out of town.
8. I plan to _____ when we get to my uncle's house.
9. My four cousins are named _____.
10. They don't live near a volcano, but they do live near _____.

Circle the preposition in each sentence.

11. Do you have any snacks in your pack?
12. I left the nuts and raisins at home.
13. I need fuel after four o'clock.
14. Put some peanut butter on this cracker.
15. This will hold you until dinnertime.

■ A **preposition** is a word that relates a noun to another word or phrase in the sentence.

■ A **prepositional phrase** contains at least a preposition and a noun. It may contain other words that modify the noun, such as articles and adjectives.

■ Some common prepositions are **to, in, on, under, of, for, from, across, between,** and **behind**.

Write a preposition from the box in each blank.

across	between	under	from	behind

16. Is that a snake's tail _____ your foot?
17. You better not look _____ you.
18. Can you swim all the way _____ the lake?
19. Never stand _____ a mother bear and her cubs.
20. I got this backpack _____ an old woodsman.

Part C

Writing a Research Report

Read the facts in this outline. Then answer the questions below.

Topic: Frogs

    I. The Life of a Frog

       A. A frog begins life as an egg in water.

       B. A tadpole hatches from the egg.

       C. The tadpole grows legs, loses its tail, and learns to breathe air.

    II. The Body of a Frog

       A. Most frogs have long, powerful back legs.

       B. Most frogs have thin, wet skin.

       C. A frog's eyes bulge out, letting it see what's all around it.

       D. Few frogs live longer than six or seven years.

1. Which item is out of place in the outline? Underline it.

2. Where in the outline would you put this detail?

Frogs have teeth in their upper jaw.

  Ⓐ under the numeral I   Ⓒ in place of The Body of a Frog

  Ⓑ under the numeral II   Ⓓ in a new section called The Teeth of a Frog

3. If you were going to write a report based on this outline, how many paragraphs would you include?

  Ⓐ one   Ⓒ three

  Ⓑ two   Ⓓ four

Put an X by each of the things you would do when writing a research report. Put an O next to each of the things you would not do.

4. _____ Write it based only on what I already know

5. _____ Include my own opinions, beliefs, and feelings

6. _____ Write an outline before I write the report

7. _____ Revise and proofread the report

8. _____ Find facts from many different sources

Adjectives and Adverbs

Part D

Draw a line under each adjective. Circle each article.

1. I saw a small green frog in the pond.
2. A big bird with a sharp beak was after it.
3. An animal in the wild has a difficult, dangerous life.
4. It was the frog's lucky day.
5. It swam under a dark rock, and the unlucky bird gave up.

Write a or an before each noun.

6. _____ beak
7. _____ oak tree
8. _____ toadstool
9. _____ harbor
10. _____ hour

Draw a line under the adverb in each sentence.

11. Dan and I walked softly through the woods.
12. He suddenly raised his arm and pointed.
13. Two deer grazed contentedly in a clearing.
14. We saw the same pair yesterday.
15. They bolted swiftly into the woods.

Write an adverb from the box in each blank.

carefully	gently	sadly	outside	today

16. _____ my brother Jack found a baby raccoon.
17. He _____ wrapped it in cloth.
18. He carried the baby raccoon _____.
19. I told him to leave the raccoon _____.
20. Jack _____ admitted that the baby was too wild to keep.

■ An **adjective** describes or tells about a noun.

■ **A, an,** and **the** are special adjectives called articles.

■ Use **a** before a word that begins with a consonant sound. Use **an** before a word that begins with a vowel sound.

■ An **adverb** can describe the action of a verb.

■ Adverbs can tell **how, when,** or **where** about an action, or they can give other information.

■ Many adverbs are formed by adding **ly** to adjectives. They often tell how; for example, **swiftly, diligently**.

■ Some adverbs do not end in **ly**. They often tell when or where; for example, **today, outside**.

Introduction

Czech author Franz Kafka's most famous short story begins with this sentence:

> "As Gregor Samsa awoke one morning from uneasy dreams he found himself transformed in his bed into a gigantic insect."
> —from *Metamorphosis*

After reading this sentence, thoughts like the ones below might pop into your head. Draw a line from each sentence to the kind of response it is.

I would just **hate** waking up as a bug!   • a question

Life is so uncertain—you never know what will happen next.   • a feeling

Will Gregor's family still care about him, or will they sell him to a traveling circus?   • a thought

As the story turns out, things do not go well for Gregor. His family is disgusted by his new identity. They try to care for him, but deep down they start to hate and fear him. The end of the story is very sad. But the ending makes readers think about the limits of love and the weaknesses of human nature. Like all good stories, this story causes readers to think, to question, and to feel.

See It Your Way
You may be asked to write about a story in a class or for a test. There is often no right answer to a question about literature. However, there **are** good and bad answers. Good answers usually include a reader's thoughts about events and characters in the story. Knowing **how** to write about literature will help you express your own special view of what you read.

In Chapter 6, you will learn how to use the language of literature to do these things:

- sum up what happened in a story
- write a personal response to a story
- compare two stories
- think and write critically about what you read

LESSON 41   Writing a Story Summary

Story Introduction

The story on the next few pages takes place on the other side of the world, on an island that is now part of New Zealand. Long ago, the Maori people paddled canoes across the South Pacific and settled on the island. They called their home "Land of the Long White Cloud." In those early times, battles often took place between native peoples. Many stories have been told about these battles. This story is a **legend**—a tale based on a real event. In it, a young Maori woman proves her courage and strength as she tries to save her people.

The Heroine of Kapiti
Retold by Shirley Climo

Like a school of flying fish, the swimmers skimmed across the water. Then one pulled ahead of the rest with such strong and smooth strokes that her arms scarcely ruffled the surface of the sea.

"Te Rau has won!" called a young girl who was watching the race from the beach. She hugged the baby she was carrying and ran with her to the water's edge.

Te Rau waded to shore, shaking the salty water from her long black hair. She picked up her feather cloak and pulled it about her wet shoulders. Then she took the baby from the excited girl.

"Are you pleased with your mother, my child?" she asked. Her daughter just snuggled against the soft feathers of Te Rau's cloak and closed her eyes.

The girl danced around Te Rau, scuffing the sand with her toes. "I am pleased," she announced, "and proud to be your sister." She looked scornfully at the other swimmers, mostly men and boys, who were just now coming ashore. "You are the best swimmer on Kapiti Island. Perhaps in all the ocean!"

Te Rau laughed. "The ocean is large; and you forget *mango,* the shark."

"Don't speak of sharks!" cried the girl, catching hold of Te Rau's hand. "I wish I were as brave as you."

Te Rau put her arm around her sister. "Then you must open your eyes to what you can do," she said, "and close your ears to those who would keep you from trying."

Te Rau knew that others were not so pleased with her swimming feat. Some of the men she had beaten grumbled as they passed her. Some of the old women who sat by the sea, soaking the leaves of the **flax** bush to soften them for weaving, shook their heads.

flax a plant that can be made into thread or cloth

"Boldness doesn't become a woman," called one, loudly enough that Te Rau might hear.

"Such foolishness is not fitting," agreed another.

"There is a **proverb**," said a third. "A fish in water; a woman on land." Then she added more kindly, "Come, Te Rau, you have played the part of fish. Now learn to weave flax."

"So I shall, soon enough," replied Te Rau, smiling down at her sister, "but there are other skills to practice too."

Then the women muttered among themselves. Te Rau's ways were **brash**, and the old women no longer thought of her as one of their people. She had married a young warrior from the North Island of Aotearoa, four miles away. Now his people and home were hers as well. She had returned to the village to visit her father, Chief Te Rauparaha. He would choose the right name for her baby daughter—just as he had called her Te Rau-o-te-Rangi, or "The Leaves of the Sky," because her hair was as dark as the midnight sky and her voice as true as the bellbird that sings at dawn.

Now Te Rau looked away from the women and up at the sky. Already the sun was slipping toward its ocean bed. So she climbed the tangled path through the trees to her hut, where she put the baby down upon her mat of ferns.

"Now you, too, must rest," she said to her sister, "for sleep brings strength."

The girl shook her head and shivered, though no breeze blew the woven reeds of the walls.

"What troubles you?" asked Te Rau.

"Take me back with you to Aotearoa," begged her sister. "I don't want to stay on Kapiti."

"This is your home," answered Te Rau, "and I cannot return until my little one is named."

"**Misfortune** comes here," whispered the girl. "I know it. For three nights I have had a dream, and it is always the same. Evil beings come by sea and turn the waters red. The wind carries the sounds of their wails." Her voice rose, and the baby stirred.

"Sssh!" warned Te Rau. "The god of the sea is our friend. The red of your dreams is but the sun reflected on the water; the cries you hear are no more than the calls of gulls."

Then Te Rau sat, cross-legged, upon the floor and softly sang an ancient charm to quiet her daughter and her sister:

"O eyes that see

be you closed in sleep,

tightly sealed, in sleep, in sleep…"

Lulled by the singing, the children slept; but Te Rau was restless and strangely troubled by her sister's words. She left the hut to walk along beside the sea. The men had long since left their games, and the women had gone to uncover their earthen ovens for the evening meal. Waves licked lazily against the shore, and the hills of distant Aotearoa looked little larger than pebbles. However, when the moon climbed into the sky, its light showed dark shapes moving silently upon the sea.

"**Porpoises**," said Te Rau aloud. "They, too, race with one another."

porpoises sea animals that look like dolphins

She stood still, watching them. Then—suddenly—Te Rau realized these were not ocean creatures at all. War **canoes** floated upon the waves, waiting for daybreak to attack Kapiti.

canoes long, narrow boats made from hollowed-out logs

Te Rau ran to give warning. Hushed and fearful, the villagers gathered at the shore and stared at the shadows on the sea. Dozens of canoes dotted the water, and each held eighty warriors. Without help from Aotearoa, the people of Kapiti would be destroyed.

Chief Te Rauparaha picked up his club. "I cannot spare a man to go for help," he said. "Every warrior is needed to protect the *pa*, the fort. We must do the best we can."

"Spare a woman," urged Te Rau. "Let me go, Father."

The chief shook his head. "They would see even the smallest canoe—and sink it immediately."

"I shall swim."

"Aotearoa is too far and there are sharks and a strong **undertow**."

"That is so," agreed Te Rau, "but I, too, must do the best I can."

undertow a strong seaward pull caused by a wave as it washes back into the ocean

Some who heard her words raised their voices to protest, and others clicked their tongues against their teeth in disapproval. This was not woman's work. Chief Te Rauparaha slapped his club upon the earth for silence.

"Go," he said to Te Rau, "and may the god of the sea go with you."

Te Rau hurried back to her hut. Both children were still sound asleep.

"Grow strong; grow brave," she whispered to her sister.

Then Te Rau looked down at her own child. She could not leave her behind. Te Rau took off her feather cloak and wrapped it about her baby. She tied it securely with thongs and hung hollow **gourds** from the lacings. Should she fail, perhaps her daughter would float safely to shore. Then Te Rau strapped her to her back, walked swiftly to the shore, and stepped into the sea.

gourds dry, hollow vegetables that look like squashes

Without a sound, without a splash, Te Rau glided past the enemy canoes. She swam strongly at first, and her baby slept as if rocked in a cradle; but as Te Rau pushed beyond Kapiti's calm lagoon, the current grew greater. Sprays of foam broke over her head, and **rip tides** tugged at her legs. Te Rau knew that she must win this race or lose her life.

rip tide a current of water that mixes with water going in another direction

Soon there was nothing to mark her way through the dark water, for mist hid both the shore behind her and the hills ahead. Then, suddenly, sea gull circled in the gray above her.

"A good **omen**!" gasped Te Rau. "The gods have sent a gull to

omen a sign of good or bad luck to come

guide me." She swam slowly, following the flight of the bird. Just as dawn reddened the clouds overhead, Te Rau felt the sands of Aotearoa beneath her feet. Struggling for breath, she shouted the alarm.

The night guards awakened the village, and at once warriors in boats set out for Kapiti. As in her sister's dreams, Te Rau listened to their cries borne upon the wind. When the battle noises ceased, she knew the war canoes had been driven off. Kapiti was safe. Only then, with her baby in her arms, did Te Rau sleep upon the sand.

Te Rau swam to save Kapiti in the year 1842. Today the island is a peaceful place, a sanctuary for gulls and other sea birds.

THINK ABOUT IT

Who is a hero you know or have read about? What did the person do to become a hero? Write some sentences about the hero and what he or she did.

Make a Story Map

A story map shows the important parts of a story in a way that is easy to understand. If you need to sum up what happened in a story, start by making a story map.

Finish the story map below.

Story Map: The Heroine of Kapiti

<u>Setting</u>   **Time:** _____

          Place: _____

                    Their Traits:

<u>Characters</u> **1.** Te Rau _____

          2. her sister _____

          3. the chief _____

          4. the other island people _____

<u>Plot</u>   **Problem:** _____

          _____

          _____

          Events:

          1. _____

          2. _____

          3. _____

          4. _____

Solution:

_____

_____

Ending   _____

_____

Write a Summary

**On the lines below, write a summary of "The Heroine of Kapiti."
Use your completed story map to help you.**

Paragraph 1:
Title, Setting,   _____
and Characters
_____

_____

_____

_____

Paragraph 2:
Plot (Problem,   _____
Main Events)
_____

_____

_____

_____

Paragraph 3:
Solution and   _____
Ending
_____

_____

_____

_____

LESSON 42   Possessive Pronouns

Try to Find It

Read these sentences. Circle the word in the second sentence that takes the place of the word in bold type in the first sentence.

> **Luke's** computer has a problem.
> His computer has a problem.

Time to Decide

Draw a line under each possessive pronoun.

1. Angus needs to take his printer into the shop.

2. Its roller makes a nasty noise.

3. I take my computer gear to Julie for repairs.

4. Her basement has become a busy work room.

5. She and her assistant keep their customers happy.

6. Is this monitor yours?

7. Mine is not working properly.

8. Our family cannot survive without computers.

9. Does your sister spend time on the Internet?

10. The pink mouse pad must be hers.

Let's Write Some

Rewrite each sentence below. Replace the words in bold type with a possessive pronoun.

11. Kamena and Andre are proud of **Kamena and Andre's** new Web site.

   _____

   _____.

12. It has flashier graphics than the Web site **belonging to my sister and me.**

   _____

   _____.

LESSON 43   Writing a Personal Response

What Did You Think?

Think about "The Heroine of Kapiti" on pages 109–112 as you answer these questions.

1. Did I like the story? Why or why not?

_____

_____

2. What did the story make me think, feel, or wonder about?

_____

_____

3. What was the best (or the worst) thing about the story?

_____

_____

4. What is the story's **theme**, or message? Do I agree with it?

_____

_____

5. Which character did I like the most? the least? Why?

Most: _____

My reason: _____

Least: _____

My reason: _____

When you write a personal response to literature, you answer questions like these. On another sheet of paper, write your personal response to "The Heroine of Kapiti." Include some of the ideas you wrote about above.

LESSON 44   More Uses of Commas

KNOW

■ A **compound sentence** is a sentence made of two groups of words that could be sentences by themselves. Use a comma before **and** or **but** in a compound sentence.

■ **Yes, well,** and **oh** can be used as introductory words. Use a comma after an introductory word.

■ A **dependent clause** has a subject and a verb but cannot stand alone as a sentence. Use a comma after a dependent clause that begins a sentence.

SPELLING BUILDER

When you make a noun plural that ends in the letter **o,** sometimes you add an **es** instead of an **s. Potatoes, tomatoes,** and **tornadoes** are words like this. Check the dictionary if you're not sure whether to add **s** or **es.**

Try to Find It

Circle the comma that separates the two parts of a compound sentence. Draw a line under the comma that sets off an introductory word. Draw a box around the comma that follows the clause beginning with although.

Yes, I am a great cook.
Although these beets look strange, they taste good.
Now I am an assistant, but someday I will be a chef.

Time to Decide

Add commas where they are needed in each sentence.

1. No that is not an avocado.

2. If you boil that milk it will spoil the pudding.

3. You peel the potatoes and I will strip the celery.

4. When you finish I will cut the potatoes into wedges.

5. Oh I almost forgot the salt.

6. Turkey is inexpensive and it has a lot of protein.

7. Yes you can barbecue a whole turkey.

8. Although lemons are sour they are used in many desserts.

9. Our guests are arriving but we are not done with the cooking.

10. Well they can make the salad.

Let's Write Some

Put the sentence parts together to write two good sentences. Use commas where they are needed.

If it rains	The party starts at 7:00	and we shouldn't be late	you should wear a slicker

11. _____

_____

12. _____

_____

LESSON 45   Writing a Comparison

Introducing Fables

A **fable** is a story that teaches a lesson. Fables usually have a **moral**—a sentence that sums up what the lesson is. The moral often appears at the end of the story. The two fables that follow were told by a traveling storyteller named Aesop, who lived about 2,500 years ago.

"The Frog and the Ox"

One day ten little frogs were playing by a pond. In a nearby meadow, an ox was eating. The ox grew thirsty and went to the pond for a drink. Its huge feet squished through the mud and crushed nine of the frogs.

The tenth frog hopped home to his mother. Sobbing, he told her that a huge beast had killed his brothers and sisters. Filled with rage, the mother frog promised to fight the beast. "The beast is much too big for you to fight!" the little frog croaked.

The mother said, "Have no fear! I will puff myself up until I am as big as the beast." She took huge gulps of air and started to puff up like a balloon. "Was the beast this big?" she asked.

"Much bigger!" cried the little frog. So the mother frog gulped more air. Soon she was as big as a bucket. "Mom, stop or you'll pop!" the frog pleaded.

The mother frog kept on gulping air. When she was as big as a boulder, she popped. The little frog cried as he stood over her remains. An older frog who had seen the whole thing sadly shook his head. "It is foolish to try and be something you are not," he said.

"The Donkey and the Lap Dog"

Once upon a time, a man owned a donkey and a lap dog. The donkey lived in a warm stable filled with clean, sweet hay. It was well fed and lovingly cared for. Each morning it went to work in the fields, and each night it returned to the stable to rest.

The lap dog did nothing but frisk around and play. When it jumped up on the man's lap, he petted it lovingly. When it licked the man's face, he fed it bits of cake. The more the lap dog frisked and played, the more the man seemed to love it.

The donkey saw this and became angry. It said to itself, "I work all day, but I sleep in a barn and eat hay. That spoiled little mutt plays all day, and it eats cake and gets petted. I think I'll try frisking around and see what it gets me."

The next day, instead of going out to the fields to work, the donkey ran around in circles and jumped over hedges. Then it trotted into the man's house, jumped onto his lap, and licked his face.

The man leaped up in anger. He smacked the donkey and marched it to the field for a long day of extra-hard work. Tired and sore, the donkey thought, "What a dumb idea that was. From now on I'll do what I was born to do, and be happy with what I have."

Think About the Fables

Answer these questions about the fables on pages 117–118. Fill in the correct circles.

1. How are the two stories alike? Choose two answers.
   - Ⓐ They are fables told by Aesop.
   - Ⓑ They give facts about animals.
   - Ⓒ They have happy endings.
   - Ⓓ They teach lessons about life.

2. How are the characters in the stories alike? Choose two answers.
   - Ⓐ They pick a foolish way to solve a problem.
   - Ⓑ They overcome a challenge.
   - Ⓒ They learn that crime doesn't pay.
   - Ⓓ They are animals.

3. What is the moral of "The Frog and the Ox"?
   - Ⓐ Slow and steady wins the race.
   - Ⓑ Oxen should watch where they step.
   - Ⓒ Do not try to be something you're not.
   - Ⓓ It is foolish to gulp air.

4. What is the moral of "The Donkey and the Lap Dog"?
   - Ⓐ Do the job that is right for you.
   - Ⓑ Cake is for lap dogs, hay is for donkeys.
   - Ⓒ Actions speak louder than words.
   - Ⓓ It is foolish to frisk around.

5. Both of these morals have to do with _____.
   - Ⓐ being kind to others
   - Ⓑ using wits to outsmart enemies
   - Ⓒ being who you are
   - Ⓓ getting what you want

6. The frog and the donkey learn similar lessons. Even so, the two characters meet very different fates at the end of the fables. In what way is this true?

Ⓐ The frog remembers the lesson, but the donkey forgets it and gets crushed by an ox.

Ⓑ The donkey lives on to apply what he learned, but the frog dies as a result of her mistake.

Ⓒ The frog gets rich, but the donkey loses everything.

Ⓓ The donkey finally gets his wish, but the frog gulps air until she pops.

Compare the Fables

Fill in the chart below to compare the two fables.

	"The Frog and the Ox"	"The Donkey and the Lap Dog"
Kind of story	7.	8.
Characters	9.	10.
Problem	11.	12.
How the characters try to solve the problem	13.	14.
How the story ends	15.	16.
And the moral is…	17.	18.

On another sheet of paper, write a comparison of the two fables. Use the completed chart and your answers to questions 1–6 to help you. The questions below will help you organize your comparison.

In this Paragraph…	Answer these questions…
Paragraph 1:	• What two stories are you comparing? (Give the titles.) • In what ways are these stories alike? • How are the characters in these stories alike? • How are the morals alike?
Paragraph 2:	• How are the characters in the two stories different? • How are the problems the characters try to solve different? • The stories end differently. How?
Paragraph 3:	• Which story did you like better? Why? (Give a personal response.)

LESSON 46   Dialogue

KNOW

- A **direct quotation** gives the exact words a person said.

- Put quotation marks around a speaker's exact words.

- Begin each direct quotation with a capital letter.

- Place end punctuation inside the end quotation mark.

- Use commas or end punctuation to separate a direct quotation from the rest of the sentence.

WRITING TIP

When writing dialogue, sometimes you can substitute a more specific word for said, such as **agreed, yelled, shouted, whispered,** or **called**. Doing this will make your writing more fun to read.

Try to Find It

Circle the sentences that give a speaker's exact words.

> Reggie said that he would wait for Ida.
> "She may not show up," said Lena.
> "When is she supposed to come?" Toivo asked.

Time to Decide

Add correct punctuation to each direct quotation. Two sentences are not direct quotations.

1. Have you heard from Shammon? asked Reggie

2. Yes, he's going over to Brooke's house said Lena

3. Brooke told me that she was going to Willie's Reggie said

4. Lena called Willie and asked Are people coming to your place?

5. I hope not Willie replied

6. He explained that his little sister had the flu.

7. I want you to help me with my math Lena said to Willie.

8. I'm better at math than Willie is said Reggie loudly

9. You are in your dreams! yelled Willie

10. Just then Reggie got a call from Brooke who said that everyone was meeting at Edna's apartment.

Let's Write Some

Rewrite these sentences as direct quotations. Use correct punctuation.

11. Reggie said that he would be there quickly.

_____

_____

12. Lena told Willie to bring his math book to Edna's.

_____

_____

LESSON 47   Critical Thinking: Writing a Critical Analysis

Be a Story Critic

As a reader, you can decide what you think about a story. Ask yourself:

• Do the setting, characters, and plot make sense, or are they hard to believe?
• Do the words the author uses help me picture the characters and setting?
• How does this story compare to other stories I've read that are like it?
• Do I agree with the story's theme or message?

An **author's purpose** is the reason why an author wrote a story. A writer may want to give facts about a topic, persuade readers to do something, or teach a lesson. Thinking about an author's purpose can help you be a better critical reader.

Reread these sentences from "The Heroine of Kapiti" and answer the questions.

> Te Rau put her arm around her sister. "Then you must open your eyes to what you can do," she said, "and close your ears to those who would keep you from trying."
>
> Te Rau knew that others were not so pleased with her swimming feat. Some of the men she had beaten grumbled as they passed her. Some of the old women who sat by the sea, soaking the leaves of the flax bush to soften them for weaving, shook their heads.
>
> "Boldness doesn't become a woman," called one, loudly enough that Te Rau might hear.

1–2. Based on the passage, which of these statements would author Shirley Climo probably agree with? Choose two. Fill in the circles.

Ⓐ Young people should act just as their elders think they should act.

Ⓑ To help a community, you may need to do something that the community does not approve of.

Ⓒ People should not listen to those who try to limit them.

Ⓓ Boldness does not become a woman.

3. Why do you think Shirley Climo wrote "The Heroine of Kapiti"?

_____

_____

4. Aesop's fables are both full of wisdom and fun to read. What purpose do you think Aesop had for telling them? Fill in the circle.

Ⓐ to give facts about the animals of his time

Ⓑ to amuse people while teaching important lessons

Ⓒ to convince people to become writers

Ⓓ to keep old legends alive

Write a Critical Analysis

On the lines below, write a critical analysis of one of the stories you have read in Chapter 6. The questions below will help you organize your writing.

In this Paragraph...	Answer these questions...
First paragraph:	• What story are you writing about? (Give the title.) • Who is the author? (Give the author's name.) • What is your overall opinion of the story? (Good or bad? Why?)
Second paragraph:	• What was the author's purpose? • Did the author do a good job of meeting that purpose? (Tell why or why not.) • Is there anything the author could have done better? If so, what?

5–6. _____

_____

_____

_____

_____

_____

_____

_____

_____

_____

LESSON 48   Troublesome Words

Try to Find It

Circle the word in bold type that means "belonging to it." Draw a line under the word in bold type that means "you are." Draw a box around the word in bold type that means "in that place."

- **It's** not a good idea for the cat to use the table leg as **its** scratching post.
- **You're** welcome to let **your** dog play in the yard.
- The birds over **there** are pretty, but **they're** not good singers.

Time to Decide

Circle the correct word in parentheses.

1. (It's, Its) exciting to be opening a new business.

2. (Your, You're) our first customer.

3. You should have a pet in (your, you're) life.

4. Pets are fun, and (their, they're, there) not expensive.

5. Dogs can give (their, they're, there) masters protection as well as affection.

6. A cat proves (its, it's) value when it catches a mouse.

7. I see that (you're, your) interested in those hamsters.

8. We have more over (their, they're, there) in the corner.

9. That gerbil and (its, it's) cage are on sale.

10. If you keep (their, they're, there) tanks clean, tropical fish will live for a long time.

Let's Write Some

Write a sentence using its, and a sentence using it's.

11. _____

_____

12. _____

_____

KNOW

■ **They're** is a contraction for the words **they are**. **Their** means "belonging to them." **There** means "at or in that place."

■ **You're** is a contraction meaning "you are." **Your** means "belonging to you."

■ **It's** is a contraction made of the words **it** and **is**. **Its** means "belonging to it."

Part A

Review Literary Terms

Write each literary term from the box next to its meaning.

legend	fable	dialogue	proverb	moral	author

1. the person who wrote a story _____
2. a short tale that teaches a lesson _____
3. the words story characters say to each other _____
4. direct statement of a fable's lesson _____
5. a well-known saying _____
6. a story about an event from long ago _____

Complete each sentence with a literary term from the box.

heroine	characters	traits	setting	theme	plot	author's purpose	events

7. The _____ in this fable include a foolish donkey and a clever crow.
8. The _____ of the story is a small town in the 1700s.
9. As part of the _____, the characters have to solve a riddle.
10. Many odd _____ lead up to the story's ending.
11. In my favorite story, a girl is the _____ who saves the day.
12. Her character _____ include bravery and courage.
13. I think the _____ for writing the story was to inspire readers.
14. I like stories whose _____ is helping others.

Possessive Pronouns and Troublesome Words

Part B

Circle each possessive pronoun.

1. That helmet is mine.

2. I think the kneepads are yours.

3. Let's take our skateboards to the park.

4. I think your left wheel is broken.

5. No, its screws are just a little loose.

■ Possessive pronouns take the place of possessive nouns such as **children's** and **Samantha's**.

■ Possessive pronouns that come before a noun are **my, your, our, their, his, her,** and **its**.

■ Possessive pronouns that stand alone are **mine, yours, his, hers, theirs,** and **ours**.

Rewrite each sentence below. Replace the word or words in bold type with a possessive pronoun.

6. Is that **Robert's** new skateboard?

_____

7. **The skateboard's** color is too wild for me.

_____

8. I like **Gwen's** idea for a skateboarding handbook.

_____

9. It was **Dana and Robert's** idea.

_____

10. Well, then, the credit is **Dana and Robert's**.

_____

■ **They're** is a contraction for the words **they are**. **Their** means "belonging to them." **There** means "at or in that place."

■ **You're** is a contraction meaning "you are." **Your** means "belonging to you."

■ **It's** is a contraction made of the words **it** and **is**. **Its** means "belonging to it."

Circle the correct word in parentheses.

11. Are (there, their) any fables in that book?

12. No, (its, it's) a book of legends.

13. I see (your, you're) studying Rome in school.

14. That must be (your, you're) history book.

15. What Roman building is on (its, it's) cover?

Write a sentence using each word.

16. its _____

17. it's _____

18. there _____

19. their _____

20. they're _____

Part C

Writing About Literature

Write a word from the box next to the description of each kind of writing.

summary	comparison	personal response	critical analysis

1. This tells how two stories are alike and different. _____
2. This tells how a reader felt about a story. _____
3. This retells the most important events in a story. _____
4. This gives a reader's judgment of whether a story was good. _____

Read this fable. On the lines below, write a personal response to it.

"The Boy Who Cried Wolf"
—Aesop

Long ago there lived a boy whose job was watching over a flock of sheep. The boy was often bored with his work. One day he thought of a joke that would make his job more fun.

Late on a quiet evening, when the village was asleep, the boy yelled "HELP! WOLF!" in a terrified voice. The people of the village came running with sticks in their hands, ready to drive the wolf away.

The sight of the frightened villagers running in their nightclothes gave the boy a good laugh, though the villagers were not amused. The boy played the same trick the next night and the next. Each time, villagers came running and the boy laughed.

On the fourth night, a wolf really did come. As it crept toward the flock of sheep, the terrified boy yelled "HELP! WOLF! REALLY!" This time no one came running to help. The wolf ate every sheep in sight.

5–10. _____

_____

_____

_____

_____

Commas and Dialogue

Part D

Add commas where they are needed in each sentence.

1. I like all fables but my favorite is "The Tortoise and the Hare."
2. Yes that story teaches an important lesson.
3. When the tortoise challenges the hare to a race everyone laughs.
4. The hare starts out fast but he gets lazy.
5. Oh I remember now that the tortoise wins!

Add the correct punctuation to each quotation. One sentence does not have a direct quotation.

6. Do you know the story of the lion and the mouse? Renna asked Nick.
7. Yes it proves that bigger isn't always better Nick said.
8. I forgot what happened first Nick said.
9. Well, a lion caught a mouse and was about to eat it Renna began.
10. Nick said That's right. Now I remember.
11. Taj added, Right! The mouse begged the lion to let it go.
12. The mouse promised it would do the lion a favor one day Taj said.
13. Renna pointed out that the lion just laughed.
14. Nick said One day the lion got trapped in a net.
15. Guess who freed him by chewing through the ropes? Renna said.

Rewrite these sentences as direct quotations.

16. The lion said that he was grateful.

_____

17. Renna asked Nick if he knew any other fables.

_____

18. Nick said that he had just finished a whole book of them.

_____

19. Renna asked Nick which story he liked best.

_____

20. Nick told her that he liked them all.

_____

- Use a comma before **and** or **but** in a compound sentence.
- Use a comma after an introductory word such as **and, or,** or **but.**
- Use a comma after a dependent clause that begins a sentence.

- Put quotation marks around a speaker's exact words.
- Begin each direct quotation with a capital letter.
- Place end punctuation inside the end quotation mark.
- Use commas or end punctuation to separate a direct quotation from the rest of the sentence.